Cambridge Elements ≡

Elements in Shakespeare and Text
edited by
Claire M. L. Bourne
The Pennsylvania State University
Rory Loughnane
University of Kent

SHAKESPEARE BROADCASTS AND THE QUESTION OF VALUE

Beth Sharrock
University of Warwick

Shaftesbury Road, Cambridge CB2 8EA, United Kingdom

One Liberty Plaza, 20th Floor, New York, NY 10006, USA

477 Williamstown Road, Port Melbourne, VIC 3207, Australia

314–321, 3rd Floor, Plot 3, Splendor Forum, Jasola District Centre, New Delhi – 110025, India

103 Penang Road, #05–06/07, Visioncrest Commercial, Singapore 238467

Cambridge University Press is part of Cambridge University Press & Assessment, a department of the University of Cambridge.

We share the University's mission to contribute to society through the pursuit of education, learning and research at the highest international levels of excellence.

www.cambridge.org
Information on this title: www.cambridge.org/9781009418003

DOI: 10.1017/9781009417990

© Beth Sharrock 2025

This publication is in copyright. Subject to statutory exception and to the provisions of relevant collective licensing agreements, no reproduction of any part may take place without the written permission of Cambridge University Press & Assessment.

When citing this work, please include a reference to the DOI 10.1017/9781009417990

First published 2025

A catalogue record for this publication is available from the British Library

ISBN 978-1-009-41800-3 Paperback
ISSN 2754-4257 (online)
ISSN 2754-4249 (print)

Cambridge University Press & Assessment has no responsibility for the persistence or accuracy of URLs for external or third-party internet websites referred to in this publication and does not guarantee that any content on such websites is, or will remain, accurate or appropriate.

Shakespeare Broadcasts and the Question of Value

Elements in Shakespeare and Text

DOI: 10.1017/9781009417990
First published online: February 2025

Beth Sharrock
University of Warwick

Author for correspondence: Beth Sharrock, elizabethasharrock@gmail.com

ABSTRACT: This Element investigates the framing 'texts' of Shakespeare's works in live theatre broadcasts produced by the Royal Shakespeare Company (RSC). Despite growing engagement from scholars of digital Shakespeares with the phenomenon of broadcast theatre and the aesthetics of filmed productions, the paratexts which accompany the live-streams – live or pre-recorded features, including interviews and short films – have largely been ignored. The Element considers how RSC live broadcasts of rarely performed, often critically maligned works are mediated for contemporary audiences, focusing on *The Two Gentlemen of Verona* (2014), *Titus Andronicus* (2017), and *The Merry Wives of Windsor* (2018). It questions the role of the theatre institution as a powerful broker in the (re)negotiation of hierarchies of value within Shakespeare's canon. Individual sections also trace the longer genealogies of paratextual value-narratives in print, proposing that broadcast paratexts be understood as participating in a broader history of Shakespearean paratexts in print and performance.

KEYWORDS: publishing, printing history, history of the book, Shakespeare, English literature – Renaissance and early modern to 1700

© Beth Sharrock 2025

ISBNs: 9781009418003 (PB), 9781009417990 (OC)
ISSNs: 2754-4257 (online), 2754-4249 (print)

Contents

    Introduction: 'This Goodly Frame'   1

1   Young and Free: *The Two Gentlemen of Verona* (2014)   18

2   Alt-Shakespeare: *Titus Andronicus* (2017)   38

3   Fictions of Composition: *The Merry Wives of Windsor* (2018)   59

    Conclusion: 'What Is Aught, but as 'Tis Valued?'   76

    Appendix: *The Two Gentlemen of Verona* (2014) Broadcast Transcript   81

    References   86

Introduction: 'This Goodly Frame'

For Alexander Pope, to assemble and present to readers a 'complete' works of Shakespeare was to own 'that with all these great excellencies, he has almost as great defects'.[1] Beyond this caveat in the Preface, the extent to which Pope gave rein to his own aesthetic judgement is notorious: large passages of the dramatic works of Shakespeare and his collaborators were relegated to the footnotes of his 1725 edited *Complete Works*.[2] These passages, lamented but not completely omitted by Pope, occupy a paradoxical space in his volumes. They are characterised by a form of inclusion – albeit a marginalised one. Within the limits of Shakespeare's complete works and legitimised by the trappings of the edited collection itself, passages maligned by Pope are positioned nonetheless on the page in a space of relative isolation: the framing 'notes' presented underneath the centrally occupying text. The spaces Pope chose to assert, challenge, and negotiate the value of these passages were paratextual.

This Element takes up questions posed by Pope's edition – how are marginal spaces used to negotiate the value of canonically marginal plays? And what is the role of the mediator in negotiating that value? – and asks these of a medium entirely alien to the eighteenth-century poet and editor. Just as the development of editorial practice was inherently tied to the publication of Shakespeare and Milton's works in the late seventeenth and eighteenth century, this study centralises a contemporary medium which has been shaped by, and has shaped, the performance of Shakespeare's plays.[3] This performance mode is the live theatre broadcast (sometimes called a 'livecast' or 'simulcast'). The term denotes a theatre performance

---

[1] Alexander Pope, 'The Preface of the Editor', in William Shakespeare, *The Works of Shakespear in Six Volumes, Collated and Corrected by Former Editions, By Mr Pope*, 6 vols., ed. Alexander Pope (London: Jacob Tonson, 1725), I: I–XXIV, iv. Titular quotation is William Shakespeare, *Hamlet, Prince of Denmark*, ed. Philip Edwards (Cambridge: Cambridge University Press, 2019), 2.2.282.

[2] Michael Caines, *Shakespeare and the Eighteenth Century* (Oxford: Oxford University Press, 2013), 33–53.

[3] Pascale Aebischer and Susanne Greenhalgh, 'Introduction: Shakespeare and the "Live" Theatre Broadcast Experience', in *Shakespeare and the 'Live' Theatre*

which is performed live in a theatre and streamed simultaneously into cinemas. Names for this hybrid performance medium abound and can hinge variously on the contexts of production (as in 'live *theatre* broadcast'), reception (as in 'live *cinema* broadcast'), or even a particular phenomenological quality (as in '*event* cinema'), while denoting the exact same context of mediated performance.

It is worth pausing briefly here to consider terminology. Live theatre broadcasts as yet lack an established critical vocabulary and methodological frameworks through which to understand how performances are presented to cinema audiences, as well as to distinguish between the various forms of 'live' stream through which that performance is distributed. This study, for example, will eschew discussion of broadcasts which composite multiple recordings of a live performance and distribute these for cinema release. Instead, the focus will be in favour of broadcasts which are performed in front of a live theatre audience, recorded and cast to cinema audiences watching in real time. In this regard, I attempt to develop but also to further delineate the definition of 'live theatre broadcast' proposed by Pascale Aebischer and Susanne Greenhalgh.[4] Their definition also encompasses 'Encore' screenings, where a live-captured production is

---

Broadcast Experience, eds. Aebischer, Greenhalgh and Laurie E. Osbourne (London: Arden Bloomsbury, 2017), 1–16. For the centrality of Shakespeare's works in the development of editorial practice in the eighteenth century, see Andrew Murphy, *Shakespeare in Print: A History and Chronology of Shakespeare Publishing*, 2nd ed. (Cambridge: Cambridge University Press, 2021); Marcus Walsh, 'Editing and Publishing Shakespeare', in *Shakespeare in the Eighteenth Century*, eds. Fiona Ritchie and Peter Sabor (Cambridge: Cambridge University Press, 2012), 21–40 and *Shakespeare, Milton, and Eighteenth-Century Literary Editing: The Beginnings of Interpretive Scholarship* (Cambridge: Cambridge University Press, 1997); Simon Jarvis, *Scholars and Gentlemen: Shakespearean Textual Criticism and Representations of Scholarly Labour, 1725–1765* (Oxford: Oxford University Press, 1995); and Margareta de Grazia, *Shakespeare Verbatim: The Reproduction of Authenticity in the 1790 Apparatus* (Oxford: Oxford University Press, 1991).

[4] Aebischer and Greenhalgh, 'Introduction', 4.

streamed asynchronously into cinemas.[5] This type of broadcast is not included here as it often features different paratextual material to the synchronously streamed broadcast.

The two most prominent producers of live theatre broadcasts in the UK, the National Theatre (NT) and the Royal Shakespeare Company (RSC), were both founded on the principle of performing Shakespeare's works and preserving the playwright's cultural legacy. They are also particularly instrumental in shaping and recirculating ideas of the playwright's cultural status to British and broader Anglophone audiences. The development of these companies' live theatre broadcasting work has provided opportunities for innovation, as well as the potential to disseminate those narratives of Shakespeare's value to larger audiences than ever before.

Since the National Theatre's debut live theatre broadcast in 2009 (NT Live), and following the emergence of the RSC's broadcasting arm, *RSC Live from Stratford-upon-Avon* (RSC Live), in 2013, these two companies have been responsible for the overwhelming dominance of Shakespearean performance in the UK's event cinema marketplace. The decade between 2009 and 2019 saw an average of four Shakespeare broadcasts produced and streamed into cinemas per year.[6] On average, then, live theatre broadcasts of Shakespeare plays were produced and distributed much more frequently than major feature film also released to cinemas in this period.[7] The number of Shakespeare broadcasts from

---

[5] Aebischer and Greenhalgh, 'Introduction', 4.

[6] Between NT Live and RSC Live, a total of forty-two broadcasts of Shakespeare's plays were streamed live into cinemas in this period; not including 'as-live' broadcasts which stream recorded performances asynchronously.

[7] The International Movie Database (IMDB) lists film and television adaptations which credit William Shakespeare as a 'writer'. Of these, eight in the period between 2009 and 2019 were feature films certified for mass release in cinemas: *The Tempest* (2010, dir. Julie Taymor); *Gnomeo and Juliet* (2011, dir. Kelly Asbury); *Coriolanus* (2011, dir. Ralph Fiennes); *Much Ado About Nothing* (2012, dir. Joss Whedon); *Romeo and Juliet* (2013, dir. Carlo Carlei); *Cymbeline* (also released under the title *Anarchy*, 2014, dir. Michael Almereyda); *Macbeth* (2015, dir. Justin Kurzel); *Ophelia* (2018, dirs. Claire McCarthy and Mørk Truvor).

these two companies also ballooned within the decade. Compared against just the one broadcast of *All's Well that Ends Well* in 2009 (from NT Live), in 2019 five productions were broadcast live into cinemas and an additional two released in pre-recorded versions.[8] The growth of live theatre broadcasts – and consequently, of the digital paratexts which accompany performances – in the UK is thus inextricably linked with Shakespeare's works. However, the role of the theatre institution in framing Shakespearean performance in this new medium is critically neglected. Just as ideas of the figure of the 'editor' in eighteenth-century England emerged largely around, and through, the publication of Shakespeare's works, Shakespeare has proven a central figure to the formation and formalisation of conventions of the live theatre broadcast medium.[9]

This study focuses on the body of live theatre broadcasts produced by RSC Live, asking how Shakespeare's works are packaged and presented to cinema audiences as part of a structured and mediated experience. These broadcasts offer a clear point of comparison with the theatrical performances they document: while the Shakespearean performance is experienced in real time by both in-house audiences and cinema audiences (albeit with significant levels of filmic mediation in the case of cinema reception), it is only in the latter context that this performance is framed by a nexus of supplementary digital features. Generally, it is these simultaneous live theatre broadcasts which tend to have the most comprehensive paratextual structures, mixing live and pre-recorded segments with live footage and audio from inside the theatre space.

---

[8] In 2019, NT Live broadcast a live production of *Richard II* from the Almeida Theatre and released a pre-recorded performance of *A Midsummer Night's Dream* from the Bridge Theatre. RSC Live broadcast productions of *As You Like It*, *The Taming of the Shrew*, *Measure for Measure*, and *Timon of Athens*; the latter production, from the Swan Theatre, was pre-recorded.

[9] For Shakespeare's role in the development of the UK's broadcast cinema market, see *Shakespeare and the 'Live' Theatre Broadcast Experience*; and *Shakespeare Bulletin* 32.2 (2014).

Figure 1 RSC Live broadcast presenter, Suzy Klein, delivering an opening monologue for the company's broadcast of *The Two Gentlemen of Verona*. © RSC.

The Element encompasses a range of prefatory paratexts to Shakespearean live theatre broadcasts: these are defined as the features and live segments broadcast prior to the beginning of the theatre performance. In the body of broadcasts produced by the RSC, presenter monologues (in which the RSC's mainstay presenter, Suzy Klein, addresses cinema audiences; see Figure 1), live or prerecorded interviews (often with the production's theatre director or with other creatives), and pre-recorded short films are typical of the kind of framing which precedes a performance.[10] Each of these three forms of prefatory broadcast paratext features in this study, and they are often considered in conversation with each other. It is these peripheral features which, this Element proposes, ought to be understood as paratextual.

[10] Beth Sharrock, 'Framing Shakespeare in New Digital Canons: Paratextual Conventions of RSC Live and NT Live', *Shakespeare Bulletin* 40.2 (2022): 239–265.

In his influential study, Gérard Genette defined the paratext as liminal and transactional: 'between text and off-text'.[11] The paratext represents 'a zone not only of transition but also of *transaction*: 'a privileged place of pragmatics and strategy ... at the service of a better reception for the text'.[12] In this description, these framing elements are integral not only to a better reception of the text but to its materialisation and legitimisation *as* a text. The paratext, Genette states, is an 'instrument of adaptation'.[13] Paratextual features 'surround [the text] and extend it, precisely in order to *present* it, in the usual sense of this verb but also in the strongest sense: to *make present*, to ensure the text's presence in the world'.[14] This function of the paratext has particular significance when applied to live theatre broadcasts, whereby the event of the theatrical performance is made more visible for geographically disparate audiences. It is typically the broadcast's supplementary interviews and live shots from the theatre interior which testify to the temporal presentness of the live performance. As Martin Barker commented of early live theatre broadcasts, such features are 'important for the "guarantee" they provide of the event's simultaneity'.[15] Just as the paratext is partly what enables the *text* to become a *book*, broadcast paratexts are also 'instrument[s] of adaptation'.[16] They are what distinguishes the theatre broadcast from the asynchronous recording – what enables the performance to be presented and legitimised as 'present' to cinema audiences.[17]

There is a precedent for critical studies which have appropriated Genette's terminology of the paratextual function. Such studies, which apply Genette's characterisation of the paratext to Shakespearean texts and to the early modern playbooks from which they originate, have shown the malleability of how paratexts function. However, these studies have also proven the reluctance of (early modern) drama to be recorded in

---

[11] Gérard Genette, *Paratexts: Thresholds of Interpretation*, translated by Jane E. Lewin (Cambridge: Cambridge University Press, 1997), 2.

[12] Genette, *Paratexts*, 2. [13] Genette, *Paratexts*, 408.

[14] Genette, *Paratexts*, 1, emphasis original.

[15] Martin Barker, *Live to your Local Cinema: The Remarkable Rise of Livecasting* (London: Palgrave, 2014), 13.

[16] Genette, *Paratexts*, 408. [17] Genette, *Paratexts*, 1, emphasis original.

a form which can be contained within Genette's parameters of 'the text'.[18] In the first instance, the fossilisation of a performance into a printed playbook risks flattening the interactivity and dynamism which characterises live performance. This is especially true of the clown figure in early modern performance who, as Richard Preiss suggests, embodied a spirit of 'unscriptedness'.[19] Moreover, as Tiffany Stern has argued, the fixity of the terms 'text' and 'paratext' are antithetical to the fluidity of early modern performance, in which any one play is 'made out of passages of variable permanence'.[20] While Genette's characterisation of the relationship between 'text' and 'paratext' has proven useful to many interested in the commercial relationship between early modern printers, playing companies, and their audiences, the framework has rarely been applied without significant caveats.[21]

Live theatre broadcast paratexts differ from bookish paratexts in two distinctive ways. The first is that, unlike printed books, broadcast paratexts unfold over a specific and set amount of time. Second and closely related is the fact that broadcast viewers have limited ways of exercising their

---

[18] For example, see Sonia Massai, 'Shakespeare, Text and Paratext', *Shakespeare Survey* 62.1 (2009): 1–11; Massai and Thomas Berger, *Paratexts in English Printed Drama to 1642*, 2 vols. (Cambridge: Cambridge University Press, 2014); Tiffany Stern, *Documents of Performance in Early Modern England* (Cambridge: Cambrdige University Press, 2009); Evelyn Tribble, *Margins and Marginality: The Printed Page in Early Modern England* (Charlottesville: University Press of Virginia, 1993).

[19] Richard Preiss, *Clowning and Authorship in Early Modern Theatre* (Cambridge: Cambridge University Press, 2014), 10.

[20] Stern, *Documents of Performance*, 255.

[21] For example, see Hannah August, 'Text/Paratext', in *Shakespeare / Text: Contemporary Readings in Textual Studies, Editing and Performance*, ed. Claire M. L. Bourne (London: Arden Bloomsbury, 2021), 50–66; Lukas Erne, *Shakespeare and the Book Trade* (Cambridge: Cambridge University Press, 2013), 90–114; Helen Smith, '"Imprinted by Simeon such a signe": Reading Early Modern Imprints', in *Renaissance Paratexts*, eds. Helen Smith and Louise Wilkinson (Cambridge: Cambridge University Press, 2011), 17–33.

autonomy over engagement with these paratexts compared with readers. Viewers cannot typically skip, rewatch, or pause in the moment: instead, audience members wishing to watch their paratexts selectively have only the option of leaving the cinema or disengaging (though, of course, etiquette might deter a viewer from holding a conversation or scrolling on their phone instead).

No theatrical programme was given to cinema viewers which delineated the exact structure of the broadcast in the examples discussed here, though each was advertised with a start time which accounted for the prefatory paratextual material rather than a start time that coincided with the beginning of the theatre performance. Genette's study has attracted critique for his tendency to imagine an ideal reader who dutifully engages with the supplementary material of a book in order. Ultimately, the relative autonomy with which a reader may pick up, put down, or skim through a book is far greater than the structured and cumulative experience typically imposed upon cinema audiences by the 'event' nature of the broadcast, and by the conventions of the cinema as a setting.[22]

Broadcast paratexts occupy not so much a transitional *space* as a transitional *time* in the wider broadcast as an ephemeral live event. This contingent quality of broadcast paratexts, and the frequency with which they are excised from archival recordings and later DVD releases, naturally invites comparisons with what scholars have found of early modern dramatic paratexts. For example, Tiffany Stern suggests that the term 'paratext' is more applicable to texts such as playbills and arguments, which circulated around the performance of a play, than to the often disordered or incomplete 'patchy' structure of many early modern playtexts which post-dated performance.[23] The comparison here with the live event of the broadcast versus its archival afterlife is instructive: where paratexts often occupy significant moments and facilitate important transitions during the span of

---

[22] Rachael Nicholas, 'Encountering Shakespeare Elsewhere: Digital Distribution, Audience Reception, and the Changing Value of Shakespeare in Performance' (Doctoral Thesis, University of Roehampton, 2019).

[23] Stern, *Documents of Performance*, 255.

the broadcast, their rate of retention in later iterations of the filmed production is typically poor.[24]

Records of a production available to stream on other platforms or purchase as a DVD may use the same recording captured for the live broadcast but the paratexts that framed the event itself in cinemas are almost universally removed or relocated as optional special features. Theatre companies like the RSC and NT Live may repackage elements of these digital performances for distribution in other forms, trimming and reordering the original live-edited transmission of the broadcast. Just as playbills and arguments were typically deemed unnecessary to the printed version of an early modern playtext, live theatre broadcasts and their afterlives are subject to similar kinds of contingency.

Moreover, broadcasts which are streamed simultaneously have a precarious liveness. Any technical errors evident in the live broadcast are liable to be edited away in later versions made for archival or commercial release. For example, the live feed for NT Live's 2011 *King Lear* was interrupted for a number of minutes on the broadcast night, but this technical fault is excised completely in the current archival version.[25] Similarly, an error which delayed the transmission of a pre-recorded interview in RSC Live's *Othello* (2015) is not retained in the DVD or digital iterations of that production available for public viewing.[26]

The implications this has for studies of Shakespearean performance in live theatre broadcast are significant and far from hypothetical: over the course of compiling the present study, the full archival versions of RSC Live's broadcasts – ones that included the framing paratexts and glitches – were removed in order to be re-archived (potentially, as attempts to recover

---

[24] Sharrock, 'Framing Shakespeare', 240–241.

[25] National Theatre Live [hereafter NT Live], *King Lear*, directed for the screen by Robin Lough, Olivier Stage at the National Theatre, London (1 Apil 2014). Accessed in the National Theatre Archive, 1 August 2018.

[26] RSC Live from Stratford-upon-Avon [hereafter RSC Live], *Othello*, directed for the screen by Robin Lough, Royal Shakespeare Theatre, Stratford-upon-Avon (25 August 2015). Private archival copy accessed with permission of John Wyver, RSC Director of Screen Productions.

the full transmissions seem to indicate, with their broadcast paratexts excised). When live theatre broadcast paratexts are not retained, it is tempting to draw on other textual witnesses to fill the gap. These might be theatrical programmes, cast lists available at cinema screenings, or, as in this study, a written transcript of a broadcast paratext. What these supplementary records lose, however, are the nuances and cadences of human speech, mannerisms, facial expressions that the filmed paratexts capture.

A partial transcript of *The Two Gentlemen of Verona* broadcast discussed here is included to give greater context to the discussion in this Element (see Appendix), though the loss of these materials during writing means that these are incomplete. In the form of a written transcript, it inevitably reproduces only part of the paratexts as broadcast, with the visual framing, sound, and many other non-verbal features not properly represented. However, this transcript attempts to give a kind of materiality to these paratexts, whose ephemerality is less a result of their perishability (like many documents associated with early modern performance) than one of limited and reduced access. The appendix to this Element thus offers a tentative appeal for the interpretive importance of these occasional performance materials. However, they also testify to the lacunae which are left by the tendency not to retain them: that is, to be treated as *purely* occasional and therefore, it seems, disposable after the fact.

*

Shakespeare's artistic and aesthetic value (largely dictated in criticism, education, and through *text*) and Shakespeare's manifest economic value (largely maintained by the distribution of his plays through *performance*) are bound in a reciprocal loop.[27] As Kate McLuskie and Kate Rumbold have highlighted, the activities of theatre companies often involve circulating and

---

[27] As Andrew Murphy has observed, there is a 'mass-market' for the publication of Shakespeare's works in the twenty-first century. This includes editions published by theatre institutions such as the RSC. Murphy notes that *The RSC Shakespeare Complete Works*, published with Macmillan, was 'presented as a tie-in' with the company's Complete Works Festival under the directorship of Michael Boyd, culminating in 2007. In Murphy, *Shakespeare in Print*, 316; see also

sustaining these forms of value in different ways.[28] Of course, these two ways of assessing value are always intertwined. While I highlight several forms and narratives of value in the discussions which follow, a common thread is how the commercial value of 'Shakespeare', the brand name in a popular medium like live theatre broadcasts, is inherently tied to the perceived value of his dramatic works in criticism, education, and within a more nebulous Anglophone cultural economy.

Attention to questions of value in textual studies of Shakespeare's works has tended to focus on a 'marketing' function of the paratext to attract potential readers – particularly in relation to the prominence (or lack) of Shakespeare's name on early printed title pages and in prefatory materials of the First Folio.[29] This study follows the work of Hannah August and Harry Newman, advocating for a return to questions of how paratexts might 'influence or guide a reception of a text and create expectations' and help us to understand 'where Shakespeare begins and ends, ... how editors locate the edges and corners of single-author canons'.[30] It is not simply editors who are doing this canonising work, though, as this Element maintains: their means of negotiating canonical boundaries are deeply comparable to those used by theatre institutions. Pursuing these same questions, then, this Element applies these paratextual frameworks instead to the strands of Shakespeare's cultural value circulated and recirculated through live theatre broadcasts.

Broadcasts and their paratexts produced by RSC Live – the branch of the broader Royal Shakespeare Company responsible for its live-to-cinema

---

Jonathan Bate, 'The RSC Complete Works Festival: An Introduction and Retrospective', *Shakespeare* 3.2 (2007): 183–188.

[28] Kate McLuskie and Kate Rumbold, *Cultural Value in Twenty-First Century England: The Case of Shakespeare* (Manchester: Manchester University Press, 2017).

[29] See Lukas Erne, *Shakespeare and the Book Trade* (Cambridge: Cambridge University Press, 2013).

[30] Hannah August, 'Text/Paratext', *Shakespeare / Text*, ed. Claire M. L. Bourne (London: Arden Bloomsbury, 2021), 50–65, 50; and Harry Newman, 'Paratexts and Canonical Thresholds', *Shakespeare* 13.4 (2017): 313–317, 313.

productions – are inherently tied to the institutional authority, branding, and even the history of the RSC itself. John Wyver, Director of Screen Productions at the RSC and Executive Producer of RSC Live, has argued that live-to-cinema broadcasts are becoming 'increasingly significant to the RSC's relationships with its audiences'.[31] Indeed, the role of paratexts within a medium which aims to broaden audience access to the company by streaming to cinemas nationally and internationally has made broadcasts an integral means by which the RSC performs what James Steichen calls 'institutional dramaturgy', that is, the process of staging its activities for audiences.[32] By extension, broadcasts have become increasingly important in shaping the Shakespearean brand upon which the RSC relies.

Of course, ideas held by a cinema audience member about either Shakespeare or the RSC are not influenced solely by the RSC's 'self-documentary' acts in the form of broadcast paratexts.[33] Stephen Purcell notes the extent to which audiences will 'inevitably arrive ... with certain preconceptions' about a performance of Shakespeare and their role within it.[34] These preconceptions may also extend to William Shakespeare as an authorial figure or brand, in line with Genette's conceptualisation of the paratext as 'the conveyor of a commentary that is authorial or more or less legitimated by the author'.[35] For UK cinema audiences, it is RSC Live's producers and screen directors who embody this 'authorial' function, projecting the RSC's role as an institution deeply tied to the continual reproduction of 'Shakespeare' the brand and cultural commodity.[36]

---

[31] John Wyver, *Screening the Royal Shakespeare Company: A Critical History* (London: Arden Bloomsbury, 2019), 183.

[32] James Steichen, 'HD Opera: A Love/Hate Story', *Opera Quarterly*, 27.4 (2011): 443–459, 446; John Wyver, 'Screening the RSC Stage: The 2014 Live from Stratford-upon-Avon Cinema Broadcasts', *Shakespeare* 11.3 (2015): 286–302.

[33] Steichen, 'HD Opera', 446.

[34] Stephen Purcell, *Shakespeare and Audience in Practice* (London: Ardem Bloomsbury, 2013), 47.

[35] Genette, *Paratexts*, 2.

[36] Genette, *Paratexts*, 2; see also Kate Rumbold, 'Brand Shakespeare?', *Shakespeare Survey* 64 (2011): 25–37.

In spite of their ephemerality, live broadcasts constitute important Shakespearean productions not least for their ability to attract sizeable audiences. NT Live's broadcast of the Barbican Theatre's *Hamlet* (2015), starring Benedict Cumberbatch in the title role, recorded a simultaneous audience of almost a quarter of a million cinemagoers and generated a total revenue in UK cinemas of £2.93 million.[37] Cumberbatch's speech calling for relief to aid asylum seekers in the European refugee crisis – a staple of the theatre production's final curtain call – became an unconventional terminal paratext to the broadcast when the actor directly addressed cinema audiences and screenings included a caption directing viewers to a dedicated Save the Children donations page. The example of *Hamlet* illustrates that not only is live theatre broadcast a medium with the potential to make big business out of Shakespeare; it is also a medium in which paratextual elements have the capacity to communicate wide-reaching narratives of value. These narratives may impact an audience member's understanding of the worth and purpose of Shakespeare's works, or the theatre company which presents them. Alternatively, as in the case of Cumberbatch's call for humanitarian aid at the conclusion of *Hamlet* broadcast, they may create a more intangible association between Shakespeare and a particular set of values or beliefs. They may, as do the case studies presented in this Element, effect a negotiation of the value of individual works which perpetuates or challenges established hierarchies in Shakespeare's dramatic canon.

The programme of broadcasts produced by RSC Live since its debut in 2013 offers a unique opportunity to explore the role of broadcast paratexts in mediating value hierarchies in and around Shakespeare's dramatic canon. As a medium founded on the adaptation of one performance and spectatorial mode (theatre) into another (cinema), live theatre broadcasts are apt to

---

[37] Rebecca Hawkes, 'Live Broadcast of Benedict Cumberbatch's *Hamlet* Watched by 225,000 People', *The Telegraph* (21 October 2015), www.telegraph.co.uk/theatre/what-to-see/benedict-cumberbatch-hamlet-live/ [accessed 3 March 2023]; David Hutchison, 'Benedict Cumberbatch *Hamlet* Takes £3m at NT Live Box Office', *The Stage* (9 December 2015), www.thestage.co.uk/news/benedict-cumberbatch-hamlet-takes-3m-at-nt-live-box-office [accessed 3 March 2023].

be analysed as the kind of 'mutually reinforcing' efforts of production which Michael Dobson notes have been integral to Shakespeare's canonisation.[38] The company's first broadcast, of *Richard II* on 13 November 2013, signalled the start of an ambitious project to mark the beginning of Gregory Doran's Artistic Directorship. Doran pledged to stage and broadcast a mainhouse production of each of the plays printed in the 1623 First Folio (and *Pericles, Prince of Tyre*: a play that did not appear in this first edition of Shakespeare's collected plays) between 2013 and 2023.[39] Though the final programme of productions and broadcasts would be significantly disrupted by restrictions imposed in the UK to curb the Covid-19 pandemic, the period of nearly eight years between *Richard II* and the temporary closure of the theatre in March 2020 nonetheless saw the company live broadcast twenty-four of the planned thirty-seven titles.

The company's broadcasting venture was thus conceived as a canonising project, rooted in the consolidation of particular types of Shakespearean value. In the first instance, Doran's plan was inherently invested in the authority of the First Folio (though, as the inclusion of *Pericles, Prince of Tyre* and exclusion of *The Two Noble Kinsmen* suggests, this authority was selectively flexible according to the commercial priorities of the company). That the First Folio provided the raison d'etre for the RSC's stage and broadcast programming from 2013 onwards at once reifies the status of this particular edition as a source of contemporary Shakespearean authority and reverence and frames the RSC's broadcast programming as a comparable canonising project of its own. In pledging to bring these productions to broader audiences and create a comprehensive digital record of the First Folio plays in performance, the goals of RSC Live reinforced the company's founding ethos of dedication to the preservation of Shakespeare's works according to the canonical parameters set by this textual record. In mounting a digital canonisation project of his own, Doran positioned himself and

---

[38] Michael Dobson, *The Making of the National Poet: Shakespeare, Adaptation, and Authorship, 1660–1769* (Oxford: Oxford University Press, 1994), 5.

[39] See Wyver, *Screening*, 2, 159–60, 183; and Peter Kirwan, 'Not-Shakespeare and the Shakespearean Ghost', *The Oxford Handbook of Shakespeare and Performance*, ed. James C. Bulman (Oxford: Oxford University Press, 2021), 87–103, 90.

the broader company as successors to the preserving role that Shakespeare's actor friends Heminges and Condell themselves assumed in the First Folio prolegomena. Doran and the RSC even scheduled the company's programme to culminate in the quatercentenary of the book's publication.

While the First Folio offered a powerful symbol of Shakespearean authority to legitimise the company's expansion into live broadcasting, adherence to this textual record of Shakespeare's works presented distinct commercial challenges for the company. Mounting a main-stage production of each of the First Folio titles required the company to schedule commercial stalwarts alongside plays which, in some instances, had not received a full, main-stage production by the company in over forty years. Closer attention to the RSC's history of programming illustrates these challenges. The company's most frequently performed plays are also largely those which also occupy other forms of canonical security and centrality: including *Hamlet* (16), *King Lear* (16), *A Midsummer Night's Dream* (17), *Romeo and Juliet* (19), *The Tempest* (18), and *Twelfth Night* (19).[40] As Will Sharpe observes, these more culturally ubiquitous works are accepted to be of Shakespeare's sole authorship.[41] They frequently appear on Anglophone school curricula (perhaps the missing candidates from the RSC's most frequently performed plays, by this criterion, are *Macbeth* and *Julius Caesar*) and are characterised by a sizable leading dramatic role(s). Their forms of material and cultural reproduction are varied, as these works tend to be frequently reproduced in printed editions for study and staging purposes; they have been adapted in film or other media; they are characterised by set pieces or stage images which may have iconographic significance associated with 'Shakespeare' the cultural commodity; and they feature prominently and favourably in the critical history of the playwright's works.

---

[40] This figure encompasses the RSC's mainhouse and Swan Theatre programming between 1960 and March 2020. See Colin Chambers, 'Appendix: Productions 1960–2002/3', *Inside the Royal Shakespeare Company: Creativity and the Institution* (London: Taylor and Francis, 2004), 192–231. Productions from 2003 to 2020 were collated by the author using archives of the Shakespeare Birthplace Trust.

[41] Will Sharpe, *Shakespeare and Collaborative Writing* (Oxford: Oxford University Press, 2023), 1.

If these conditions outlined above may be thought of as markers of value and canonical security typical of the RSC's most frequently performed plays, the company's least frequently performed works are similarly characterised by the absence of these criteria. The three case study broadcasts covered in this Element – *The Two Gentlemen of Verona*, *The Merry Wives of Windsor*, and *Titus Andronicus* – exemplify the challenges of attracting theatre and cinema audiences to lesser known and arguably less valued plays. Of the 24 plays which received a live broadcast into cinemas, these three were among the least frequently performed in the RSC's history. While the primary focus of this Element is the paratextual framing of contemporary performances, individual sections will trace the longer genealogies of imparting value to the plays through textual examples since Shakespeare's death – with a particular focus on the editorial and adaptive energies of Shakespeare editions in the late seventeenth and eighteenth centuries. Approaching the ways in which this marginality was signalled to, and mediated for, contemporary cinema audiences, I also consider how the value of these works has been negotiated at different stages of – to use Emma Depledge's term – Shakespeare's 'rise to cultural prominence'.[42] Understanding how these plays have been evaluated in historical print paratexts to these plays is instructive for understanding their framing for contemporary audiences. Each play was positioned by the RSC in a degree of contrast to long-standing narratives of Shakespeare's cultural value. It is the contention of this study, then, that these modern and digital materials should be set in conversation with the historical print examples which participated in the development of the value-narratives recirculated by later broadcast paratexts.

Section 1 begins with the RSC's first season of live theatre broadcasts by examining the paratexts of Simon Godwin's production of *The Two Gentlemen of Verona* (2014) alongside the notes to Samuel Johnson's edition of the play in his collected *Plays of William Shakespeare* (1765). *The Two Gentlemen of Verona* was one of the earliest broadcasts produced by the company, so it makes good sense that the framing of this production in

---

[42] Emma Depledge, *Shakespeare's Rise to Cultural Prominence: Politics, Print and Alteration, 1642–1700* (Cambridge: Cambridge University Press, 2018).

cinemas was also markedly interested in the value of Shakespearean 'novelty' as well as being evidently anxious about the status of *The Two Gentlemen of Verona* as an apparently 'novice' work. This section thus isolates two forms of paradoxical value sought by the company and by Johnson's edition when framing the play. The first is the merit of *The Two Gentlemen of Verona* as both focused on youthful behaviour within its fiction and as an insight into an artistically immature Shakespeare; and the second is the freedom that the play's relative lack of performance precedents offers to directors and actors when contrasted with Shakespeare's more canonically central, and frequently staged, works.

In Section 2, I explore how the broadcast of *Titus Andronicus* (2017) appropriated the shock-value and extremity typically used to market the performance of plays by Shakespeare's contemporaries, while simultaneously and conspicuously avoiding discussions of the play's co-authorship. How is *Titus Andronicus*, a play whose violent excesses critics and directors have traditionally been reluctant to endorse as Shakespeare's, positioned for contemporary audiences in the context of a canonising project to which Shakespeare as author is foundational? This question is pursued through a discussion of the broadcast's paratextual appeal to an 'alternative' Shakespeare and through comparison with the framing of Edward Ravenscroft's Restoration adaptation, *Titus Andronicus: or, the Rape of Lavinia* (performed 1678, printed 1687). I consider how both examples of the play's paratextual mediation draw on a sense of counter-cultural allure, radical relevance, and subversive appeal which stands in opposition to the playwright's own position at the centre of mainstream British culture.

The third and final section turns to the ways in which broadcast paratexts imagine Shakespeare at work, with an analysis of the RSC's *The Merry Wives of Windsor* (2018). I suggest that, in foregrounding of the myth that *The Merry Wives of Windsor* was written to a hasty royal commission in a live interview before the performance, this broadcast anticipates and attempts to excuse deficiencies in the play which it seems shy of identifying outright. I compare this use of the commission theory to its iterations in an adaptation by John Dennis (*The Comical Gallant: Or, the Amours of Sir John Falstaffe*, 1702) and a prefacing *Account* of the life of Shakespeare in Nicholas Rowe's collected edition of 1709. Implicit in RSC Live's framing of *The Merry Wives of Windsor*, I argue, is the recirculation of a familiar, Romantic notion of authorship and an older history of investing in different forms of biographical narrative: that Shakespeare's most accomplished works (which do not include this parochial comedy) are the result of the playwright operating above and outside of the commercial conditions of the late sixteenth- and early seventeenth-century playhouses.

The conclusion reflects on what is to be gained – and, perhaps, lost – from analysing these materials as functioning 'paratextually'. I suggest that a closer attention to how works at the fringes of Shakespeare's canon are framed for mainstream cinema audiences yields important insights into the role of the RSC as theatre institution. In turn, the Element proposes that these digital performance materials and the institutional agents who create them prompt us to revisit and re-evaluate the desires and value judgements which shape Shakespeare's paratexts in print.

1 Young and Free: *The Two Gentlemen of Verona* (2014)

When the RSC broadcast its production of *The Two Gentlemen of Verona* (hereafter *Two Gentlemen*) on 3 September 2014, the event was a novelty thrice over. Firstly, there had not been a full-length production of *Two Gentlemen* in the Royal Shakespeare Theatre, the company's mainhouse, in forty-four years. This fact was reiterated emphatically by presenter Suzy Klein in her welcome to cinema audiences and again in a pre-show short film by the production's stage director, Simon Godwin.[43] Secondly, this broadcast of *Two Gentlemen* followed and departed from the company's recent focus on a series of closely connected productions: *Richard II* (broadcast 9 November 2013), *Henry IV, Part I* (broadcast 14 May 2014), and

[43] Time stamps will be provided for quotations from the RSC's broadcast of *The Two Gentlemen of Verona*. Unfortunately, due to loss of access to the broadcasts of *Titus Andronicus* and *The Merry Wives of Windsor*, these will not be provided in citations for these broadcasts. [Presenter Monologue] RSC Live, *The Two Gentlemen of Verona*, directed for the screen by Robin Lough, Royal Shakespeare Theatre, Stratford-upon-Avon (3 September 2014): 00:05:42; [Pre-Show Short Film], RSC Live, *The Two Gentlemen of Verona*: 00:13:31.

Henry IV Part II (broadcast 18 June 2014).[44] And, thirdly, where this triad of Shakespeare's histories had been performed by an ensemble cast which shared roles across the productions, a new (and notably young) cast for *Two Gentlemen* meant a stage populated with fresh faces.

The company's debut season of live theatre broadcasts thus charted a course away from a cycle of linked productions and the commercial draws of David Tennant in the role of Richard II, and Antony Sher as Falstaff in the two *Henry IV* plays towards a play which, as the broadcast itself was keen to emphasise, had not been seen in the Royal Shakespeare Theatre in nearly half a century. Given that the RSC's Artistic Director Gregory Doran had directed these three preceding history plays, *Two Gentlemen* would be the first in the company's nascent broadcasting programme not to have involved Doran as a stage director. In a medium like live broadcast that is so heavily reliant on translating the onstage grammar and rhythms dictated by the theatrical director, and in method of production which consults these directors regularly, *Two Gentlemen* offered an opportunity for distinction and experiment.[45]

This section considers how the RSC's broadcast of *Two Gentlemen* positioned the play itself as a novelty and an experiment. Prefatory paratexts to the broadcast identified two paradoxical strands of value in the play: its status as a rarely performed Shakespearean work, and its novice-like quality as an early-career one. The RSC Live broadcast of *Two Gentlemen* illustrates how the RSC's broadcast producers could invert the commercial instability of Shakespeare's less frequently performed works. Rather than a potentially risky venture, the play was presented in this broadcast as refreshingly nascent and freed from the weight of performance precedents. Underlying the paratextual focus on the fact that *Two Gentlemen* had not been seen in the RSC's main theatre since 1970, however, was the need to address a potentially inconvenient truth. The corollary to *Two Gentlemen*'s

---

[44] While Shakespeare's two *Henry IV* plays are typically rendered as *1 Henry IV* and *2 Henry IV*, I have here used the stylised *Part I* and *Part II* to replicate how these plays were titled in the RSC's production and later broadcasts.

[45] Wyver, 'Screening the RSC Stage', 292.

novelty is the implication that play does not merit the kind of regular revival associated with others of Shakespeare's works.

Interviews with the production's stage director and cast members also highlighted the youth of the play's characters, aligning this thematic element of *Two Gentlemen* with a narrative of Shakespeare as apprentice playwright. Recently dated to 1588, *Two Gentlemen* could represent Shakespeare's earliest preserved play.[46] The cast members and director involved in broadcast paratexts to this performance were less interested in the precise chronology of the play than in considering what this earliness might mean within a broader narrative of Shakespeare's works – a narrative which typically pulls towards the association of Shakespeare's mid-career with his most accomplished works. The broadcast relied upon these implicit associations of Shakespeare's earliest works with 'reduced worth, underdevelopment, and immaturity'.[47] Nonetheless, the apparent immaturity of *Two Gentlemen* was mitigated by positioning the play as the forerunner to a number of Shakespeare's more canonically central and 'socially entrenched' plays.[48]

This section will question, on the one hand, how this paratextual framing might have anticipated the kind of engagement with Shakespeare's works described by Rory Loughnane and Andrew J. Power, whereby 'most readers of Shakespeare begin somewhere in the middle of the collected works, with super-canonical works like *Twelfth Night* and *Hamlet*, before, if ever, working to the margins of the canon where most of the early works reside'.[49] Moreover, I consider how the contradictory value of that earliness

---

[46] Gary Taylor and Rory Loughnane, 'The Canon and Chronology', in *The New Oxford Shakespeare: Authorship Companion*, ed. Gary Taylor and Gabriel Egan (Oxford: Oxford University Press, 2017), 486.

[47] Rory Loughnane and Andrew J. Power, 'Beginning with Shakespeare', in *Early Shakespeare: 1588–1594*, eds. Loughnane and Power (Cambridge: Cambridge University Press, 2020), 1–20, 6.

[48] Eoin Price, 'Canon: Framing not-Shakespearean performance', in *The Arden Research Handbook of Shakespeare and Contemporary Performance*, eds. Peter Kirwan and Kathyrn Prince (London: Arden Bloomsbury, 2021), 151–170, 151.

[49] Loughnane and Power, 'Beginning', 2.

was figured for contemporary cinema audiences. To do so, I examine the paratextual notes to *Two Gentlemen* in Samuel Johnson's *The Plays of William Shakespeare* (1765), tracing how the contention over the value of the play between editors quoted by Johnson and Johnson himself resonates with the RSC's framing of the value of the play as unpolished but appealingly raw.[50] I reckon with how ideas of youth (Shakespeare's, and that of his characters in this play) and novelty have been long been used to attenuate the apparent artistic demerits of *Two Gentlemen*. The RSC Live broadcast thus reached simultaneously for two, contradictory, forms of value: on the one hand, Shakespeare's artistic exceptionalism and the commercial security of his brand name; and on the other, an appeal to the value and fascination of a Shakespearean work which is, in some ways, still 'in progress'.

The paratextual style of the 2014 RSC Live broadcast of *Two Gentlemen* exhibited its own forms of early-canon experimentation.[51] It is, for example, the only RSC Live broadcast to feature an opening welcome from the broadcast presenter on stage with actors in character, and to conduct a live interview from inside the public spaces of the Royal Shakespeare Company building: during the interval, presenter Suzy Klein interviewed Doran in a public walkway between the company's two theatres. The broadcast's pre-show paratexts lasted approximately ten minutes and consisted of a short video montage; a presenter monologue; a pre-show short film; followed by a second monologue from Klein.

The opening montage is particularly significant for the broadcast's attempts to position *Two Gentlemen* in relation to more frequently performed Shakespeare plays. A little over thirty seconds in length, this brief montage comprised clips in which speakers in a variety of locations around the Royal Shakespeare Company's building and surrounding outdoor locations in Stratford-upon-Avon would collectively recite the phrase: 'Love, Jealousy,

---

[50] William Shakespeare, *The Plays of William Shakespeare, with the Corrections and Illustrations of Various Commentators*, ed. Samuel Johnson, 8 vols. (London: J. and R. Tonson et al., 1765).

[51] [Opening montage] RSC Live, *The Two Gentlemen of Verona*: 00.04.58–00:05:20.

Figure 2 A woman delivers a line while seated in front of the River Avon, adjacent to the Royal Shakespeare Theatre. © RSC.

Friendship, Obsession' (see Figure 2).[52] The montage would, for example, shift from a woman seated in a deck chair on the bank of the Avon saying 'Love', to a man sat in the RSC's prop department in the process of crafting a wooden prop gun reciting 'Jealousy'.[53] Speakers included a handful of the production's cast members – seen variously backstage in dressing rooms or corridors – and the RSC's own front-of-house staff, as well as members of the prop and costume departments. The role of speakers was often signified by their location or an activity they were engaged in during the short clip – in the case of actors from the production, it may have been assumed that cinema audiences would recognise them from a series of slides showing cast members and their roles which had been running prior to the scheduled start time of the broadcast. This montage is the first and only example of its kind within the RSC's body of live theatre broadcasts, suggesting not simply that this broadcast exhibits an unusual level of paratextual experimentation (which it

---

[52] [Opening Montage] RSC Live, *The Two Gentlemen of Verona*: 00.04.58–00:05:20.
[53] [Opening Montage] RSC Live, *The Two Gentlemen of Verona*: 00.04.58–00:05:20.

certainly does) but also that the play itself was judged to require an unusual level of broad thematic exposition. The four key terms – love, friendship, jealousy, obsession – were offered to cinema audiences as cardinal points by which to navigate the presumed unfamiliarity of the play. The simplicity of the terms and their repetition in different voices align this opening paratext with the mode of instruction often used to introduce students to the study of Shakespeare, whereby plays are accessed (and knowledge is often assessed) through the paradigm of a selection of themes.[54]

Sarah Olive suggests that a theme-driven pedagogical approach is a result of a critical trend for close-reading of Shakespeare's works, championed by I. A. Richards and F. R. Leavis. Olive notes that '[i]nstead of declaiming or acting Shakespeare's texts, students were increasingly required to synthesise from their teachers and play texts ... an understanding of character, theme, plot and the craftsmanship of Shakespearean language'.[55] In this way, this montage demonstrated an anxiety on the part of the RSC Live's production team about the status of *Two Gentlemen*: that this play, unlike the number of canonically central and more frequently performed Shakespearean works, required a more interventionist and pedagogically familiar form of introduction. The RSC's status as a charity with an educational remit is relevant to the way in which this broadcast, first and foremost, was concerned with filling a presumed gap of knowledge for its audiences. The almost ritualistic repetition of key words offered

---

[54] For example, the Oxford Cambridge and RSA's (OCR, which is one of the UK's largest secondary-education examining bodies) 2022 exam script for GCSE English Literature included questions on *Romeo and Juliet, The Merchant of Venice, Macbeth,* and *Much Ado about Nothing*. Students were asked to consider themes including love and hate, justice, violence, ambition, and villainy in relation to these works. Oxford Cambridge and RSA (OCR), *GCSE English Literature J352/22 Shakespeare (8 June 2022)* www.ocr.org.uk/Images/685747-question-paper-shakespeare.pdf [accessed 5 July 2023].

[55] Sarah Olive, *Shakespeare Valued: Educational Policy and Pedagogy 1998–2009* (Bristol: Intellect, 2015), 20.

cinemagoers an extremely simple set of thematic entry-points through which to engage with the production.

Moreover, this model of expository paratext relied upon the assumption that cinema audiences would be familiar with Shakespeare's more canonically central works, those which feature more regularly in the RSC's performance repertoire. The thematic tags of 'love, friendship, jealousy, obsession' could themselves by used to frame several of Shakespeare's works. Perhaps due to the ubiquity of Shakespeare's drama in Anglophone education, these terms also inevitably evoke particular plays. Love and jealousy, for example, are perhaps more likely to conjure for general audiences associations of *Romeo and Juliet* and *Othello*, two plays which appear much more frequently in mainstream UK theatres and on educational curricula than *Two Gentlemen*.

While love, friendship, jealousy, and obsession were offered here as thematic tags for better understanding the play, the montage offered no specific glossing of these themes nor textual examples through which to contextualise their significance to *Two Gentlemen* itself. This ambiguity seems to assert that the play is best approached through viewers' presumed familiarity of Shakespeare's other works. The reduction of the play to a handful of one-word themes similarly anticipates the kind of narrative unfamiliarity which audiences rarely experience in the case of some of Shakespeare's most famous works. Where a number of plays are so well-known that the idea of 'spoilers' may not apply, the *Two Gentlemen* opening montage seemed anxious to *offer* gentle narrative spoilers to help frame the play for cinemagoers.

In this way, the broadcast's opening montage laid the groundwork for associations which would be developed more fully in a pre-show short film that followed. Interviews with the production's stage director, Simon Godwin, and with four principal cast members in the roles of Valentine (Michael Marcus), Proteus (Mark Arends), Sylvia (Sarah McRae), and Julia (Pearl Chanda) furthered this framing of *Two Gentlemen* as an immature 'work-through' of Shakespeare's artistic abilities. The short film reinforced this suggestion: that the play is best understood as an immature or experimental early attempt to explore themes shown in Shakespeare's later and, by implication, more developed works. Following from a discussion of the play's characters and setting, the film introduced the focus on the play's underdeveloped quality through voiceovers from Marcus and then McRae. Narration from both actors was overlaid onto footage of the cast in rehearsal, spliced together with each actor's to-camera interviews. In Marcus's first clip, for example, his voiceover glossed fast-paced shots of the cast walking through the rehearsal space and engaging in improvised conversations with each other:

> It's been really nice to work on a play that was written by a young writer, writing about young people. It was very early on in Shakespeare's career and so you kind of see this writer who's clearly got quite profound thoughts and a really unique insight into the world and into playwriting, but in some areas has not quite developed those thoughts and ideas yet but will do throughout his career.[56]

Marcus's description of the play as a kind of rehearsal for Shakespeare's more developed works echoes much of the critical reception of *Two Gentlemen* from the nineteenth-century onwards. In 'The Failure of *The Two Gentlemen of Verona*', Stanley Wells recounts a history of critical appraisals of the play as deficient and incomplete, including Coleridge and Hazlitt's characterisations of the play as a 'sketch'.[57] In addition to collating these judgements, Wells himself issues a sustained critique of the play's demerits compared with Shakespeare's broader works. Wells's assessment, that the 'basic technical failure of the play ... arises from the fact that Shakespeare is still a tyro in dramatic craftsmanship' was reiterated implicitly by the narratives of value offered in Marcus's narration.[58]

Marcus's suggestion that the play contains early examples of Shakespeare's later 'profound thoughts and ... unique insight' represents a relatively familiar teleological narrative of Shakespeare's gradual artistic maturity

---

[56] [Pre-show Short Film] RSC Live, *The Two Gentlemen of Verona*: 00.12.32–00.12.57.

[57] Stanley Wells, 'The Failure of *The Two Gentlemen of Verona*', *Shakespeare Jarbuch*, 99 (1963), 161–173, 161.

[58] Wells, 'The Failure of *The Two Gentlemen of Verona*', 165.

towards a mid-career zenith.[59] There has historically been, as Loughnane notes, a general critical reluctance to label any of Shakespeare's dramatic works under the category of 'juvenilia'.[60] However, it is perhaps significant that the two plays identified by Loughnane which have attracted this term are the subject of this section and the next. Both *Two Gentlemen* and *Titus Andronicus*, as the term 'juvenilia' seems to suggest and these broadcasts affirm, require careful framing in order to not upset a vision of Shakespeare as unblemished, dramatic genius.

An interview clip with Sarah McRae followed, in which her narration furthered the implication that *Two Gentlemen* can (and perhaps *should*) be read as a rehearsal for Shakespeare's later works. McRae similarly emphasised the mirroring youth of Shakespeare and the play's protagonists: 'probably because he was very young when he wrote it as well, I think it is a kind of [story of] coming-of-age, growing up, and accepting what isn't perfect.'[61] Shakespeare's own age is used to create a causal link to the concerns of the play; *Two Gentlemen* is concerned with the transition from youth to adulthood 'because [Shakespeare] was very young when he wrote it'.[62] As a means of glossing the play's chronological position in Shakespeare's canon, this statement moves from tentative external evidence (i.e., Shakespeare's relative youth) to interpretive internal evidence (the youth of the play's protagonists, the *bildungsroman* quality of Valentine's journey to Milan) to establish an interdependent relationship between the two which hinges around an interest in Shakespeare as a young artist.

The coding of the play as chronologically early because of Shakespeare's youth is, of course, relative. Loughnane's analysis of the writing careers of Shakespeare alongside a number of contemporary playwrights demonstrates that, although Shakespeare's life span is roughly average,

---

[59] [Pre-show Short Film] RSC Live, *The Two Gentlemen of Verona*: 00.12.45.

[60] Rory Loughnane, 'Shakespeare and the Idea of Early Authorship', in *Early Shakespeare: 1588–1594*, eds. Rory Loughnane and Andrew J. Power (Cambridge: Cambridge University Press, 2020), 21–53.

[61] [Pre-show Short Film] RSC Live, *The Two Gentlemen of Verona*: 00.12.58–00.13.07.

[62] [Pre-show Short Film] RSC Live, *The Two Gentlemen of Verona*: 00.12.58.

his playwrighting career is longer than the average career of his peers by ten years. The result is a canon through which we can reasonably conjecture that Shakespeare 'starts [writing] earlier than average [for his peers] and ends significantly later'.[63] The caveats that define the limits of Loughnane's analysis – the relatively poor survival rate of plays prior to the 1580s, the instability of dating and authorship for plays from this period – highlight the contingency of attempts to link particular works to periods of Shakespeare's 'youth' versus 'maturity'. Nonetheless, the short film for this broadcast relied upon the imagined connection between a 'youthful' Shakespeare and the principal characters in *Two Gentlemen*. In the process of imagining Shakespeare's own age and its relationship to the play, this short film was interested in attributing to *Two Gentlemen* some of the mixed associations of juvenilia.

If the short film constructed *Two Gentlemen* as part Shakespearean run-through, part juvenilia, it also attempted to redeem Shakespeare from the associations of imperfection and immaturity that this framing carries. McRae's narration concluded with the argument that *Two Gentlemen* is ultimately about 'learning to understand, to forgive and – uhm, yeah, [learning] that things won't be perfect but that's part of growing up'.[64] In the context of the broadcast's wider framing of *Two Gentlemen* as canonically marginal, including the emphasis on its comparatively sparse performance history, the imperfection that McRae identifies as one of the play's primary concerns incorporates its critical reputation and stage history. The connection continually drawn in this short film between Shakespeare's artistic immaturity and the immaturity of the characters in *Two Gentlemen* allows for this description of the play as ultimately redemptive and accepting to extend to the apparent deficiencies of Shakespeare's art. Like the 'loss of moral coherence' and insufficient 'depth of characterisation' among the play's youthful protagonists, this section of the short film implies that Shakespeare, too, is in need of redemption.[65]

---

[63] Loughnane, 'Shakespeare and the Idea', 37.

[64] [Pre-show Short Film] RSC Live, *The Two Gentlemen of Verona*: 00.13.11–00.13.17.

[65] Wells, 'The Failure of *The Two Gentlemen of Verona*', 167.

Figure 3 Michael Marcus in rehearsal for *The Two Gentlemen of Verona*. Footage of the cast rehearsing was used in the pre-show short film to the broadcast. © RSC.

The impression that the play is 'not quite developed' was also visually enforced through shots of the cast rehearsing (see Figures 3 and 4).[66] Rehearsal games and dynamic, improvised movement sequences underscored Marcus's narration which characterised *Two Gentlemen* as a playground for Shakespeare's nascent artistic ability. The emphasis on actors rehearsing in the prefatory short film was perhaps intended to implicitly absolve Shakespeare from some of the play's sexual and romantic politics which have troubled its performance history. These include a lack of psychological plausibility in Proteus's changes of affection from Julia to Sylvia and a handful of challenges in the play's final scenes: Proteus's threat to rape Sylvia, Valentine's offer to relinquish his own affection for Sylvia and 'give' her to Proteus, and Sylvia's sustained silence throughout this

---

[66] [Pre-show Short Film] RSC Live, *The Two Gentlemen of* Verona: 00.12.46.

Figure 4 Footage of the cast in rehearsal for *The Two Gentlemen of Verona*, included in the pre-show short film to the RSC's broadcast. © RSC.

exchange.[67] Recalling the RSC's 1991 production at the Swan Theatre, Thomas Clayton notes, '[T]o the extent that [the play] itself is well known, its climactic crux ... is no less well known, since the interpretation of the play rests on resolving it, sometimes by the facile expedient of ignoring or even omitting it.'[68]

An attempt to 'resolv[e]' the play's uncomfortable and implausible plot turns may be implicit in the short film's visual emphasis on the rehearsal

---

[67] William Shakespeare, *The Two Gentlemen of Verona*, ed. Roger Warren (Oxford: Oxford University Press, 2008), 5.4.55–59; 5.4.83. Sylvia is silent for the remainder of the play following Valentine's offer to relinquish her to Proteus in this final scene (5.4.58–171).

[68] Thomas Clayton, 'The Climax of *The Two Gentlemen of Verona:* Text and Performance at the Swan Theatre, Stratford-upon-Avon, 1991', *Shakespeare Bulletin* 9.4 (1991): 17–19, 17.

room.[69] The associations of experimentation and improvisation arguably framed the performance with a kind of pre-emptive contingency: as if the play (as well as the production) were still being worked through by the cast and production team. Like Wells's assessment of Shakespeare's 'tyro ... craftsmanship', the short film's use of rehearsal footage anticipates accusations that the play's characters, their behaviours, and motivations are implausible and even reprehensible.[70]

The impulse to apologise for the quality of *Two Gentlemen*, then, was firmly couched in a biographical narrative that indulged an imagined version of Shakespeare as a young, inexperienced playwright. How broadcast paratexts engage with Shakespeare's biography to negotiate the value of marginal plays is also explored in the final section of this Element, together with how these paratexts imagine versions of Shakespeare's artistic composition. In this example, *Two Gentlemen*'s deficiencies – alluded to through its presumed unfamiliarity to audiences and its sparse performance history at the RSC – were mapped onto the image of a Shakespeare still training for the artistic maturity which characterises later plays, and particularly those thematically aligned with the play.

Turning to the play's editorial history illustrates long-standing continuities in how editors, directors, and theatre companies have approached the tensions of value inherent in *Two Gentlemen*. A similar attempt to mitigate the apparent immaturity of the play and to frame it as an appealing Shakespearean 'rehearsal' is evident in Samuel Johnson's edition of the play in *The Plays of William Shakespeare* (1765). Johnson's *Shakespeare*, financed by subscription, appeared in eight octavo volumes ten years after his initial appeal for contributions. Johnson's edition was the first of those published by the Tonson publishing syndicate to employ variorum-style discursive footnotes, which Johnson used to mount sometimes extensive glosses to the plays.[71] These notes were partly designed to replicate the end-loaded page layout of Richard Bentley's 1713 Amsterdam edition of Horace, which was also the model for Johnson's editorial predecessor Lewis Theobald in his

---

[69] Clayton, 'The Climax', 17.

[70] Wells, 'The Failure of *The Two Gentlemen of Verona*', 165.

[71] Walsh, *Shakespeare, Milton, and Eighteenth-Century Literary Editing*, 168.

1733 edition of Shakespeare's works.[72] In addition to supplying his own editorial judgements, Johnson's conspicuous change to these notes was in the way he collated and engaged with the observations of previous editors and commentators.[73] It is a variorum-style approach which would be developed further by Johnson and his collaborator, George Steevens and, in its paratextual inclusion of different critical voices, parallels the RSC's practice of including multiple actors and creatives in their broadcast interviews.[74]

Two Gentlemen appears in the first volume of Johnson's eight octavos, nestled between *A Midsummer Night's Dream* and *Measure for Measure*. The preliminary notes to each play across his edition typically propose a judgement of its quality and often draw together the opinions of other commentators; Johnson's first footnote to *Two Gentlemen* forms the focus of my discussion here. No introductory note in this first volume is as extensive nor as discursive as this note for *Two Gentlemen*. It reproduces a number of select comments from previous editors: the first is from Alexander Pope ('[*Two Gentlemen* is] supposed to be one of the first he wrote', from his 1725 edition), followed by Thomas Hanmer speculating on the play's authorship ('It may very well be doubted, whether *Shakespear* had any other hand in this play than the enlivening it with some speeches and lines here and there,' from Hanmer's 1744 edition).[75] As a gloss to introduce the play, these selected comments from Pope and Hanmer both emphasise a sense of *Two Gentlemen* as atypical, or existing outside of a particular standard expected of Shakespeare's works.

---

[72] Lewis Theobald, 'Letter to William Warburton, 18 November 1731', in *Illustrations of the Literary History of the Eighteenth Century*, 8 vols., ed. John Nicholls (London: Nichols, Son and Bentley, 1817–1858), II: 621.

[73] Samuel Johnson, 'Preface', *The Plays of William Shakespeare*, vol.1, lix; see also, Walsh, 'Editing and Publishing Shakespeare', 31.

[74] See Arthur Sherbo, 'George Steevens's 1785 Variorum "Shakespeare"', *Studies in Bibliography* 32 (1979): 241–246; Marcus Walsh, 'George Steevens and the 1778 Variorum: A Hermeneutics and a Social Economy of Annotation', in *Shakespeare and the Eighteenth Century*, eds. Peter Sabor and Paul Yachnin (Hampshire: Ashgate, 2008), 71–83.

[75] Johnson, vol. 1, 179n1.

By far the most sustained engagement Johnson makes with the view of another critic is in his effort to dismantle an observation from John Upton, taken from the latter's second edition of *Critical Observations on Shakespeare* (1746). Where Upton disputes the play's Shakespearean authorship, Johnson dissects his logic and shifts Upton's own metaphor of a painterly style instead towards the discussion of *Two Gentlemen*'s earliness:

> Mr *Upton* peremptorily determines, *that if any proof can be drawn from manner and style, this play must be sent packing and seek for its parent elsewhere. How otherwise,* says he, *do painters distinguish copies from originals, and have not authors their peculiar style and manner from which a true critic can form as unerring a judgement as a Painter?* I am afraid this illustration of a critick's science will not prove what is desired.[76]

The structure of this extensive footnote allows Johnson to prove his own 'critick's science'.[77] He challenges the equivalence made by Upton's metaphor between a painter's copy and the imitation of a painter's style, suggesting that '[c]opies are known from an original even when the painter copies his own picture'.[78] *Two Gentlemen*, Johnson then suggests, might more appropriately be considered in terms of juvenilia: 'some painters have differed as much from themselves as from any other; and I have been told, that there is little resemblance between the first works of *Raphael* and the last.'[79] By redirecting critique of the play towards juvenilia rather than co-authorship, Johnson aligns himself with Pope's earlier assessment and crucially complicates the conclusion drawn by other commentators: that the work is artistically deficient and therefore must not be authorially Shakespeare's.

In its staging of a critical debate in a footnote, Johnson's framing of *Two Gentlemen* exposes some of the anxieties implicit in the RSC's broadcast. It is perhaps significant that both paratexts centre on creative metaphor: the visual context of the rehearsal space is paralleled, in Johnson's fixation with

[76] Johnson, vol. 1, 180n1. [77] Johnson, vol. 1, 180n1. [78] Johnson, vol. 1,180n1.
[79] Johnson, vol. 1, 180n1.

Upton's metaphor of painting, by the image of the artist's studio. Accordingly, just as the RSC's short film reaches a point in McRae's narration where the earliness of *Two Gentlemen* must be brought to an uncomfortable resolution (the play is about how 'things won't be perfect'), Johnson also reaches a complex judgement of the value of the play at the end of this introductory note.[80] Though the play 'is not indeed one of his most powerful effusions', Johnson finds in *Two Gentlemen* 'both the serious and ludicrous scenes, the language and sentiments of *Shakespear*'.[81] The consonance between these two conclusions suggests that perhaps *Two Gentlemen* remains critically unresolved, or unresolvable. The play's earliness may be deeply relative and always operating in relation to assumptions of Shakespeare's elevated value, but, as Johnson's note suggests, it also offers a productive opportunity to examine and critique our own broader assumptions of artistic maturity and authorship.

Alongside the RSC's broadcast framing, which emphasised the play as an early Shakespearean 'rehearsal', was a decided focus on the novelty of *Two Gentlemen* in performance. Simon Godwin addressed the merits of the play's performance history towards the end of the short film, arguing that *Two Gentlemen* is a privileged Shakespearean work for being comparatively freed from performance precedents. In this instance, other productions in the RSC's completist project offer a unique point of comparison. Godwin directed *Hamlet* for the RSC two years after this broadcast of *Two Gentlemen*. That production, too, was streamed into cinemas and featured a prefatory live interview between Godwin and Suzy Klein in which the weight of performance history was discussed. Klein's interview with Godwin for the broadcast of *Hamlet* included a question on his approach to this much-performed play: 'I want to talk to you about ... the ghosts of productions past ... was it an intimidating prospect to do *Hamlet* for the RSC?'[82] Godwin's involvement as an interviewee in both broadcasts sharpens the contrast in his later discussion with Klein

---

[80] [Pre-Show Short Film] RSC Live, *The Two Gentlemen of Verona*: 00.13.15.

[81] Johnson, vol. 1, 180n1.

[82] [Pre-show Live Interview] RSC Live, *Hamlet*, directed for the screen by Robin Lough, Royal Shakespeare Theatre, Stratford-upon-Avon (8 June 2016).

regarding a lack of performance precedents for *Two Gentlemen*, in which he addressed the opposite concern:

> I was delighted that [the play] hadn't been done for so long because there isn't that historical baggage that can feel so intimidating: everyone comparing that production to one that they had seen the year before, or the actors knowing people that had played their own parts or carrying those kind of cultural memories. There's no baggage with this [play].[83]

This clip makes a virtue of the play's sparse performance history. Indeed, Godwin's repetition of the term 'baggage' is telling for how it serves to problematise the relatively secure value of Shakespeare's more canonically central plays.[84] *Two Gentlemen* emerges, by comparison, as a rare opportunity. It is at once attached to the commercial security of Shakespeare's brand name *and* unburdened of the performance precedents Godwin suggests can hamper the creative freedom of actors and directors.

Accordingly, the appeal of *Two Gentlemen* as a kind of Shakespearean novelty implies that there is greater space for innovation and failure than would be afforded in performances of the more culturally ubiquitous works. As Eoin Price argues, 'The rarely performed marketing tag casts the RSC, and their audience, as intrepid adventurers, rediscovering a lost classic.'[85] The culture of comparison and memory Godwin refers to is both the burden and the privilege of canonical centrality. While *Two Gentlemen* may exist on the very margins of the popular performance canon, this paratextual mediation of the play suggests that those margins of the canon are a space of comparative freedom from the weight of Shakespeare's monolithic cultural status. A framing narrative such as this is particularly complicated by the commercial model of the RSC. The company's practice of regularly

---

[83] [Pre-show Short Film] RSC Live, *The Two Gentlemen of Verona*: 00.13.33–00.13.50.

[84] [Pre-show Short Film] RSC Live, *The Two Gentlemen of Verona*: 00.13.50.

[85] Price, 'Canon', 153.

restaging Shakespeare's most popular plays arguably relies on the same 'cultural memory' which is portrayed by Godwin as a creative burden.[86] In this way, the RSC operates via a model which contributes significantly to the Shakespearean 'baggage' against which *Two Gentlemen* – and the other works discussed in this Element – can be set in opposition.[87]

The framing of the *Two Gentlemen* live broadcast illustrates the agility of the paratextual space to negotiate a thin line between lamenting a theatrical market seemingly oversaturated with a handful of Shakespeare's works and capitalising on the novelty of others. Godwin's characterisation of *Two Gentlemen* demands further attention for the way it anticipates particular types of audience engagement. Dobson argues that the RSC's 'home audience ... specialize in hoarding up enormous stores of memories', consisting of productions mounted by the company and other Shakespearean performances.[88] Of Shakespeare's more frequently performed plays, Godwin also notes how audiences 'compar[e]' individual productions, incorporating these into a web of 'cultural memories' for a play in terms which resonate with Dobson's discussion of the RSC's core audience.[89]

Back in the late eighteenth century, Johnson's paratextual note also finds real value in the play's lack of performance precedents, though for reasons which show the difference between Godwin's role as a director and Johnson's as editor. Early in his introductory note, Johnson quotes a comment from Lewis Theobald that *Two Gentlemen* is one of 'Shakespear's worst plays, and is less corrupted than any other'.[90] In the context of Theobald's critique and elsewhere in editions of this period, 'corrupted' typically refers to an anxiety

---

[86] [Pre-show Short Film] RSC Live, *The Two Gentlemen of Verona*: 00.13.49.

[87] [Pre-show Short Film] RSC Live, *The Two Gentlemen of Verona*: 00.13.50.

[88] Michael Dobson, 'Watching the Complete Works Festival: The RSC and Its Fans in 2006', *Shakespeare Bulletin* 25.4 (Winter 2007): 31.

[89] [Pre-show Short Film] RSC Live, *The Two Gentlemen of Verona*: 00.13.49; Dobson, 'Watching the Complete Works Festival', 23–33.

[90] Johnson, vol. 1, 179n1. For Theobald's edition see Peter Seary, *Lewis Theobald and the Editing of Shakespeare* (Oxford: Clarendon Press, 1990); and Carly Watson, 'From Restorer to Editor: The Evolution of Lewis Theobald's Textual Critical Practice', *The Library* 20.2 (2019): 147–171.

over errors or interventions imposed by the printers and compositors of Shakespeare's early texts. At the end of Johnson's note, he reflects that despite passages in the play that are 'eminently beautiful', he is 'inclined to believe that [*Two Gentlemen*] was not very successful, and suspect that it has escaped corruption because being seldom played it was less exposed to the hazards of transcription'.[91] The anxieties of the textual editor over the play's value are evident in Johnson's suggestion that the play had enjoyed a relatively straightforward textual history on account of its 'being seldom played'.[92] *Two Gentlemen* was not performed in an unaltered version until 1784, nineteen years after the publication of Johnson's first complete Shakespeare edition – in this regard, both Johnson's note and the RSC's broadcast fossilise a particular moment in the performance history of this play in which the value of novelty can be claimed enthusiastically.[93]

For Johnson and Theobald as textual editors – and particularly working in the eighteenth century, when editorial practice was developing significantly – *Two Gentlemen*'s relative unpopularity has important benefits. In their view, a sparse performance history for the play could be seen as valuable in that it allows for the preservation of a considerably less 'corrupt[ed]' Shakespearean work.[94] Johnson's concern with the play as comparatively untouched by the interference of printing processes also helps to offer a window into the desires and concerns of those publishing Shakespeare in the eighteenth century. The period abounds in successive collected editions of Shakespeare's works. This is partly testament not just to the industriousness of the Tonsons and legal changes occasioned by the Copyright Act of 1709, but it also reflects the participation of Shakespeare editions (and those of other English writers, Milton prominent among them) in ongoing attempts to both classicise English vernacular writers and standardise elements of the English language.[95]

---

[91] Johnson, vol. 1, 180n1. [92] Johnson, vol. 1, 180n1.

[93] Johnson, vol. 1, 180n1; Roger Warren, 1; Kurt Schlueter, 'Introduction' in William Shakespeare, *The Two Gentlemen of Verona*, ed. Kurt Schlueter (Cambridge: Cambridge University Press, 2012), 1–47, 22.

[94] Johnson, vol. 1, 180n1.

[95] See Andrew Murphy, *Shakespeare in Print: A History and Chronology of Shakespeare Publishing*, 2nd ed. (Cambridge: Cambridge University Press, 2021),

Shakespeare Broadcasts and the Question of Value 37

Johnson's completion of an English dictionary ten years prior to his Shakespeare edition, of course, solidifies this relationship between the publication of Shakespeare's works and the impulse to make these works the principal part of an 'authoritative basis on which to render the English language as pure and stable as the classical languages were considered to be'.[96] Within this broader project, Johnson's suggestion that the poor performance history of *Two Gentlemen* renders the play as perhaps the closest example of a Shakespearean original has real value: it is *because of* the play's apparent artistic deficiencies that it has escaped, in Johnson's words, 'the hazards of transcription'.[97]

In his final note to *Two Gentlemen*, Johnson returns to a contradictory statement of the play's 'strange mixture of knowledge and ignorance'.[98] He attempts to explain and resolve some of the inconsistencies in the play in his notes throughout, but he uses this final paratextual space to suggest that the challenges of *Two Gentlemen* arise from Shakespeare adapting his source material haphazardly: '[t]he reason of all this confusion seems to be, that he took his story from a novel with he sometimes follows, and sometimes forsook, sometimes remembered, and sometimes forgot.'[99] This is a different narrative of the play's provenance from that in the RSC's broadcast and is, importantly, not as concerned to connect the play to a period of Shakespeare's youth. Nonetheless, it hints at an artistic immaturity and human fallibility similar to that used to frame the RSC's broadcast: the image of Shakespeare 'for[saking]' and 'forg[etting]' the details of his source material resonates with Marcus's reflection on his '[un]developed' abilities, and McRae's argument that the play is about 'accepting what isn't perfect'.[100]

85, 101; Simon Jarvis, *Scholars and Gentlemen: Shakespearean Textual Criticism and Representations of Scholarly Labour, 1725–1765* (Oxford: Oxford University Press, 1995), 11; and Walsh, *Shakespeare, Milton, and Eighteenth-Century Literary Editing*, 116–117.

[96] Jarvis, 11.   [97] Johnson, vol. 1, 180n1.   [98] Johnson, vol. 1, 259n5.
[99] Johnson, vol. 1, 259n5.
[100] Johnson, vol. 1, 259n5; [Pre-Show Short Film] RSC Live, *The Two Gentlemen of Verona*: 00.13.15.

The framing of these two productions of *Two Gentlemen*, one in performance and one in print, suggests how this play continues to present a challenge to ideas of Shakespeare's elevated artistic ability. Johnson's interest in a lack of corruption from performance and textual transmission speaks, in an age of saturated print editions of Shakespeare's works, to the potential of *Two Gentlemen* to serve as an access point to a particular kind of 'purity'. In their respective approaches to the status of *Two Gentlemen* as an early work, too, both Johnson's edition and the RSC's broadcast attempted to mitigate fears about the standard of the play and its unfamiliarity through its apparent access to (for Johnson) an 'uncorrupted' Shakespearean text and (for the RSC) a version of the playwright in a state of embryonic artistic ability. The RSC's broadcast also used the play to respond to another form of saturation. By emphasising a dynamic, 'rehearsal' quality in *Two Gentlemen*, and the significant gap of time since the play had been staged in the RSC's main theatre, the broadcast tapped into forms of value that the company's own theatrical repertoire makes scarce. In a theatrical market oversaturated with professionalised Shakespearean performance, the incompleteness and unfamiliarity of *Two Gentlemen* allowed the play (and an image of its playwright) to appear genuinely novel to audiences.

2 Alt-Shakespeare: *Titus Andronicus* (2017)

Like *Two Gentlemen* in 2014, the RSC's 2017 broadcast of *Titus Andronicus* capitalised partly on what it means to stage an 'early' Shakespearean work.[101] Taylor and Loughnane have recently attributed the play to as early as 1589, and critical treatments of *Titus* have certainly been anxious to stress the play's status as potential juvenilia.[102] The reliance of the play on the Elizabethan schoolroom text of Ovid's *Metamorphoses* has made it apt to be branded as showing a particularly juvenile approach to dramatic composition. As Jonathan Bate and Eric Rasmussen have put it, *Titus* can read

---

[101] RSC Live, *Titus Andronicus*, directed for the screen by Matthew Woodward, Royal Shakespeare Theatre, Stratford-upon-Avon (9 August 2017).

[102] Taylor and Loughnane, 'The Canon and Chronology', 490–493.

like the work of a 'very clever, very naughty schoolboy'.[103] The RSC's broadcast similarly imagines a transgressive vision of the play's radical difference, as in the moment when David Troughton (who played Titus) remarked in a pre-show interview that 'it's like Shakespeare's on acid'.[104]

Titus has been marked as errant in moral terms, too: it features multiple brutal murders, onstage mutilations, and cannibalism. The play's sexual and racial politics have proven troubling for readers and audiences alike. It demands the graphic depiction of the aftermath of Lavinia's rape and mutilation, testing the absolute limits of theatrical representation through her severed hands and tongue. In the consistent association of Aaron's Blackness with villainy (by other characters, as well as by himself), *Titus* exploits racial stereotypes by depicting the 'nightmare of a black man with access to power'.[105] The challenges of both staging and watching *Titus* have resulted in its occupying an uncomfortable place in critical and editorial appraisals of Shakespeare's canon.

The anxiety that *Titus* is morally and canonically errant – a Shakespearean work in need of discipline – underpins many of the RSC Live broadcast's paratextual features. Stage productions always face the dilemma of not only how to represent much of its violent action and graphic spectacle, but how also to frame this for audiences. Likewise, any production which situates the play within a broader canon of Shakespeare's works must reckon with what Bate has observed as a long-standing history of critical attempts to 'find grounds for devaluing its place in Shakespeare's career or even dismi[ss] it from the canon of his works altogether'.[106] In

---

[103] Jonathan Bate and Eric Rasmussen, 'Introduction: The Lamentable Tragedy of Titus Andronicus', in *The RSC Shakespeare: The Complete Works* 2nd ed., eds. Jonathan Bate and Eric Rasmussen (London: Arden Bloomsbury, 2022), 1597–1600, 1598.

[104] RSC Live, *Titus Andronicus*.

[105] Carol Mejia LaPerle, '"If I Might Have My Will": Aaron's affect and race in *Titus Andronicus*', in *Titus Andronicus: The State of Play*, ed. Farah Karim-Cooper (London: Arden Bloomsbury, 2019), 135–156, 137.

[106] Jonathan Bate, 'Introduction', in William Shakespeare *Titus Andronicus*, rev 3rd ed., ed. Jonathan Bate (London: Arden Bloomsbury, 2018), 2–3.

a canon often defined by poetic elevation, refinement, and claims of universality, *Titus* is characterised by jolting tonal shifts between horror and humour, an aesthetic of excess, the association of moral depravity with Aaron's race, and the rape and mutilation of Lavinia.

Despite apparently testing the limits of what can comfortably be assimilated into the category of 'Shakespearean', the RSC's broadcast chose to minimise discussions of the play as a co-authored work. That is to say, *Titus* was simultaneously positioned as an 'Other' within the Shakespeare canon but *not* as a work with the influence of George Peele as co-author, as is generally accepted in critical discourse surrounding the play.[107] As the play continues to enjoy both a 'critical resurgence' and a rehabilitation in popular performance contexts, its mediation in print and performance suggests how far the play still occupies a paradoxical position in relation to narratives of Shakespeare's cultural value.[108] This section explores how *Titus* has transcended hallmarks of Shakespearean value, including the associations of his works as morally edifying and enduringly relevant, and the image of Shakespeare as a bastion of cultural traditionalism and poetic refinement.

I use the tensions of the RSC's broadcast framing as a way to explore the play's textual and adaptation history and vice versa, paying particular attention to paratextual articulations of *Titus*'s alterity. Drawing on the early Victorian print and editorial practices which helped to create the image of Shakespeare as paternalistic and moralising, I explore how the play presents a particular challenge both to this image and to its broader implications of paternal relatives using Shakespeare's works to instruct their younger, female dependents. I also examine the framing of Edward Ravenscroft's alteration of the play, *Titus Andronicus: Or, the Rape of Lavinia*, to consider the relationship between the play's aberrant morality (a source of *potential* value) and its political relevance (a source of *certain* value). Turning again and again to the RSC's framing of the play in its broadcast, I suggest that an integral part of *Titus*'s rehabilitation on the page

[107] Taylor and Loughnane discuss the play's co-authorship in 'The Canon and Chronology', 491.

[108] Farah Karim-Cooper, 'Introduction', in *Titus Andronicus: The State of Play*, ed. Farah Karim-Cooper (London: Arden Bloomsbury, 2019), 1–12, 2.

and stage for contemporary audiences is a careful and measured embrace of its difference vis-à-vis Shakespeare's more canonical and frequently performed plays. Through the emphasis on its alterity in its print and performance paratexts, *Titus* has come to occupy the status of what I term an 'alt-Shakespearean' work.

To understand how the RSC positioned *Titus*'s contradictory canonical value requires some exploration of the performance tradition of works by Shakespeare's contemporaries and the commercial appeal of not-Shakespeare. The term 'not-Shakespeare' has proven useful to critics and scholars as a way of discussing the broader corpus of early modern drama, as well as addressing the outsized predominance of Shakespeare's works within performance and reception of that dramatic corpus. It has also offered a vocabulary through which to conceptualise the performance of works by Shakespeare's contemporaries, particularly when staged by theatre institutions whose primary commercial draw is staging Shakespeare. As Peter Kirwan has highlighted, '[T]he main centres for the performance of not-Shakespeare ... are institutions dedicated to the transmission of Shakespeare.'[109] Inevitably, theatre companies frequently position their staging of works by other early modern dramatists in opposition to what they anticipate audiences might expect of a Shakespeare play – if Shakespeare's works are elevated, refined, and cerebral, productions of contemporary works are characterised by '(moral) decay, excess and violence'.[110]

Of all Shakespeare's plays, *Titus* is the one raised most frequently in studies of the performance of not-Shakespeare. Stage productions and film adaptations, as Kirwan and Pascale Aebischer and Kathryn Prince observe, have visualised the moral corruption dramatised in *Titus* through markers of apparent social deviance more typical of the staging of later, Jacobean drama.[111] For example, the leather-clad, tattooed Goths in Julie Taymor's

---

[109] Kirwan, 'Not-Shakespeare', 89; Pascale Aebischer and Kathryn Prince, 'Introduction', *Performing Early Modern Drama Today*, eds. Pascale Aebischer and Kathryn Prince (Cambridge: Cambridge University Press, 2012), 1–16, 2.

[110] Susan Bennett, *Performing Nostalgia: Shifting Shakespeare and the Contemporary Past* (London: Routledge Press, 1996), 81–82.

[111] Kirwan, 'Not-Shakespeare', 96.

1999 film and the BMX-riding teenaged Chiron and Demetrius in Michael Fentiman's 2013 production in the Swan, the RSC's second stage, suggest how this faction within the play are associated with different forms of counterculture. Stagings which emphasise a sense of hedonistic luxuriance are also common: in Selima Cartmell's 2005 production at Dublin's Project Arts Theatre, a towelled Chiron and Demetrius conspired with Aaron to rape Lavinia while receiving full-body massages, while Blanche McIntyre's production which was broadcast for the RSC staged this scene with the Goth brothers sunbathing and emerging from an in-built pool. The 'Jacobean aesthetics' of transgression, counterculture, and even conspicuous consumption have become an ingrained mode through which performances inscribe the (moral and racial) 'Otherness' of Aaron and Goth characters in the play.[112] Through this performance tradition and its close association with staging conventions for not-Shakespeare, *Titus* has been repeatedly signalled in the theatre as a subversive and canonically marginal work.

For theatre companies such as the RSC and Shakespeare's Globe, too, the relationship between Shakespeare's works and those of contemporary playwrights is often literalised through the programming of larger and smaller theatre spaces. Shakespeare's plays often dominate in the mainstage theatre spaces of the RSC and the Globe, while ancillary theatres are typically dedicated to (or may have originally been envisioned for) staging the work of his contemporaries. This division of performance spaces can frequently reinforce the relationship between Shakespeare and not-Shakespeare as one of both difference and mutual dependency.[113] For example, the RSC's 'Roaring Girls' season of 2014 staged a number of works by Shakespeare's contemporaries in the company's secondary Swan Theatre. Emma Whipday notes that the marketing of this programme capitalised on 'the stories of transgressive early modern women alongside [the mainhouse staging of] Shakespeare's history plays', positioning these works by Shakespeare's contemporaries as an 'an alternative' to the

---

[112] Ania Loomba, 'Wilderness and Civilisation in *Titus Andronicus*', *Shakespeare, Race, and Colonialism* (Oxford: Oxford University Press, 2002), 75–91.

[113] Kirwan, 'Not-Shakespeare', 89.

male-dominated, canonically central, and commercially secure histories unfolding next door.[114]

From the outset of the RSC's broadcast, and despite being staged in the company's mainhouse theatre, *Titus* was presented as a transgressive alternative to assumptions about Shakespeare's canonical works in the mould of a not-Shakespeare production. In her opening monologue to cinema audiences, presenter Suzy Klein introduced the play as 'one of Shakespeare's earliest' and 'also one of his most brutal'.[115] This description aligns chronological marginality with the play's violent extremity, figuring both through the literal extremity of language seen in the superlatives 'earliest' and 'most'. As with the company's broadcast of *Two Gentlemen*, this framing is implicated in a broader tradition of assigning typically devalued qualities – immaturity, a lack of restraint, experimentation – to the chronological category of 'early' works.[116]

This opening monologue signalled a further association of the play's earliness with its excessive violence when Klein delivered a euphemistic content warning: 'tonight's production features bloody acts and not a little gore.'[117] That the RSC felt *Titus* needed a form of perfunctory warning suggests that the levels of graphic violence which feature were not anticipated to be within the range of an audience's expectations of a Shakespeare play. However, in its coy evasion of details from the play, this introductory warning not only signals a subversion of an audience's expectations but also revels in withholding the exact nature of the play's dramaturgical transgressions. It is a form of anticipation through censorship which advertises the play's extremes of violent action as an attraction, while shying away from the exact nature of its sexualised and racialised content.

Following from this was a pre-recorded interview with McIntyre, the production's stage director. McIntyre's semi-scripted interview clips principally offered exposition of the plot and considered its relevance to contemporary audiences. Her descriptions were characterised by frequent use

---

[114] Emma Whipday, '"The Picture of a Woman": Roaring Girls and Alternative Histories in the RSC 2014 Season', *Shakespeare* 11.3 (2015): 272–285, 273.

[115] [Pre-show Presenter Monologue] RSC Live, *Titus Andronicus*.

[116] Loughnane and Power, 'Introduction: Beginning with Shakespeare', 6.

[117] [Pre-show Presenter Monologue] RSC Live, *Titus Andronicus*.

of *accumulatio*, a rhetorical technique in which adjectives or synonymous descriptions are piled in succession to create an effect of amplification. For example, McIntyre argued that the reputation of *Titus* has been skewed for contemporary audiences, largely because the play is 'so bloodthirsty and because it's so action-packed and so full of butchery'.[118] Similarly, later in the interview McIntyre characterised the accumulative structure of violent action in *Titus* in rhetorical terms which enacted this accumulation, observing that when the Roman state 'treats [marginalized groups] with violence, they respond with more worse violence and the establishment then responds with still more worse violence'.[119] Both instances frame the action of the play in terms which emphasise its violence as excessive. In the first example, the repetition of 'so' amplifies particular descriptive terms individually ('bloodthirsty'; 'action-packed'; 'full of butchery') while also gesturing towards a broader repetitive structure of violence.[120] By comparison, the second example takes this reiterative violence almost to a point of grammatical collapse: in which 'violence' becomes 'more worse violence' becomes 'still more worse violence'.[121] The effect of these superlatives and accumulative descriptions is to suggest not only that the play exceeds the bounds of effable violence, but as a result that it exists beyond what cinema audiences might expect of Shakespeare's canonically central works.

Two examples in which McIntyre begins false-start sentences, or redirects her locutions part way through, are indicative of an attempt to negotiate some of the play's particular challenges. For example, McIntyre broached a turning-point in the play which sees Titus burst into laughter at the height of his misery:

> There's something particular with *Titus* which is different –
> it's about the structure of the play – in the first few acts,
> while you care about the characters, they're very hard to
> watch because you watch with your sympathy engaged.

---

[118] [Pre-recorded Interview] RSC Live, *Titus Andronicus*.
[119] [Pre-recorded Interview] RSC Live, *Titus Andronicus*.
[120] [Pre-recorded Interview] RSC Live, *Titus Andronicus*.
[121] [Pre-recorded Interview] RSC Live, *Titus Andronicus*.

There's a moment where Titus can't take it anymore and he laughs, and as soon as he laughs it becomes possible for the audience to laugh.[122]

It is important to stress that these interview clips are semi-scripted (producers often prepare set questions which are given to an interviewee in advance), and statements prepared in response naturally exhibit this partly improvised and conversational quality. For example, another form of broken sentence appeared in McIntyre's live interview, when the director discussed Roman state violence in the play. She noted that 'there is something about the – *Titus* as a play which I find quite disturbing'.[123] Both of these instances of verbal breakdown occur when McIntyre tries to articulate a certain a quality of the play's alarming difference from audience expectation. Through these false-start sentences and moments of grammatical disruption, McIntyre's discussion of *Titus* implicitly – and sometimes explicitly – frames the play as a disturbing and disruptive 'Other' in relation to the canon.[124]

The implication that *Titus* poses a threat by exceeding a presumed Shakespearean 'limit' is also manifested across the pre-show paratexts through a particular pattern of describing the play. In interview clips with cast members, in Klein's monologues to cinema audiences, and McIntyre's interview, *Titus* was repeatedly referred to as 'extraordinary' and 'extreme'.[125] That the framing of the play should be characterised by the prefix 'ex-', with its associations of outdoing or overreaching, again reframes the violence which proved so distasteful in the play's critical history as part of its subversive appeal. In particular, 'extraordinary' recurred in three contexts and reveals much about the presumptions of an 'ordinary' Shakespeare against which this broadcast attempted to define *Titus*.[126] Klein described the play as featuring 'some of Shakespeare's most

---

[122] [Pre-recorded Interview] RSC Live, *Titus Andronicus*.
[123] [Pre-recorded Interview] RSC Live, *Titus Andronicus*.
[124] [Pre-recorded Interview] RSC Live, *Titus Andronicus*.
[125] [Pre-recorded Interview] RSC Live, *Titus Andronicus*.
[126] [Pre-recorded Interview] RSC Live, *Titus Andronicus*.

extraordinary poetry', whereas in a pre-recorded short film actors Stefan Adegbola (Aaron) and David Troughton (Titus) both used the term to express a sense of narrative incredulity.[127] Adegbola noted that Aaron 'starts off as a prisoner, um, and in an extraordinary twist of events he becomes the main man to the empress'.[128] Perhaps to avoid narrative spoilers, there is no further detail given by Adegbola about the problematic way that Aaron's change of fortune comes about. Nonetheless, this short description of Aaron's trajectory in the play participates in the broadcast's wider rhetorical trend of figuring *Titus* in terms of extremity.

Later in the short film, Troughton characterised the overall plot of the play as 'a really tragic first half and then the most extraordinary – it's like Shakespeare's on acid – he goes into the most amazing imaginative mad scenes'.[129] Troughton's interjection imagines a radically transgressive provenance for the play. The image of 'Shakespear[e] on acid' suggests that Shakespeare's most well-regarded works were composed in a state of comparative sobriety, against which Titus represents a kind of psychedelic and artistic fever dream. Moreover, this image derives humour from the play's extreme difference – just as *Titus* itself shifts discomfortingly between the extremities of tragedy and comedy through its persistent puns on hands, and through the collapse of Titus into fits of laughter in the first scene of Act 3. In place of what may have been 'an extraordinary [second half]', Troughton landed instead on a comic and transgressive metaphor which illustrates the extent to which the play apparently exists outside of a Shakespearean 'norm'.[130] This 'norm', however, was left largely undefined by the actor. The implication is that audiences would have been familiar with this sober Shakespeare, creating works whose dramatic and tonal structures are more consistent and refined than what they were about to see in *Titus*.

Though 'Shakespeare on acid' may be a tongue-in-cheek imagining of the play's composition, it exemplifies how this broadcast effected a reframing of the value of *Titus* against a presumed expectation of

---

[127] [Pre-show Short Film] RSC Live, *Titus Andronicus*.

[128] [Pre-show Short Film] RSC Live, *Titus Andronicus*.

[129] [Pre-show Short Film] RSC Live, *Titus Andronicus*.

[130] [Pre-show Short Film] RSC Live, *Titus Andronicus*.

Shakespeare's plays. In this regard, the RSC's broadcast paratexts for *Titus* were inevitably responding to the play's status as an outlier within a broader transition of sanitisation, censorship, and Bowdlerisation. Throughout the late eighteenth and early nineteenth centuries, print and performance practices shifted towards what Michael Dobson has called a 'morally pruned' Shakespeare. Dobson draws particular attention to the emergence of Shakespeare in theatrical adaptations as a sexually chastising, spectral figure.[131] In his ghostly form, 'his dangerous, errant corporeality bowdlerised away', this Shakespeare was also affected by contemporary efforts to sanitise some of the more licentious biographical anecdotes which circulated around editions of his works in the centuries after his death.[132]

Gary Taylor suggests that the prevailing association of Shakespeare (in the nineteenth century and beyond) with virtuous respectability is partly a consequence of the Bowdlers' increasingly popular anthology, which 'never chose selections [of Shakespeare's works] that would offend anyone's decency'.[133] However, Henrietta and Thomas Bowdler's *Family Shakespeare* (1807; later republished in an expanded edition in 1818) is often considered the apotheosis of this broader trend for expurgation. Molly Yarn argues that the popularity of the Bowdlers' original and subsequent editions, and of Charles and Mary Lamb's contemporary *Tales from Shakespeare*, speaks to a broader desire to use the Shakespearean text as a domestic and paternal instrument. To fully appreciate the implicit Shakespearean standard which was consistently evoked in the RSC's broadcast of *Titus*, one must also reckon with the extent to which the play poses a threat to this chastened image of the playwright and the long shadow it has cast.

As Yarn highlights, Shakespeare, as canonical and colonial father, was subject to a series of alterations which 'frame themselves in relation to

---

[131] Michael Dobson, 'Bowdler and Britannia: Shakespeare and the National Libido', *Shakespeare Survey* 46 (2007): 137–144, 142.

[132] Margareta de Grazia, *Shakespeare Verbatim: The Reproduction of Authenticity and the 1790 Apparatus* (Oxford: Clarendon Press, 1991), 75–7; and *Shakespeare without a Life* (Oxford: Oxford University Press, 2023), 17–25.

[133] Gary Taylor, *Reinventing Shakespeare: A Cultural History from the Restoration to the Present* (London: Hogarth Press, 1989), 209.

a male authority controlling access' to his works.[134] Indeed, in the preface to the expanded second edition of the *Family Shakespeare* (1818), Thomas Bowdler notes that his 'object' in publishing the expurgated plays was to enable 'a father to read one of Shakespeare's plays to his family circle ... without incurring the danger of falling unawares among words and expressions which ... raise a blush on the cheek of modesty'.[135] The first edition of Henrietta Bowdler's twenty plays does not feature *Titus Andronicus*, which appears only in the expanded second edition edited by her brother, Thomas. Principal targets for expurgation are the sexually charged exchanges between Aaron and Tamora, suggesting a particular distaste for the representation of their interracial relationship, and direct references to Lavinia's rape.

Titus occupied an uneasy place in Thomas's completist second edition. Though, as Adam H. Kitzes notes, it would be *Othello* and *Measure for Measure* which would present the greatest challenges in terms of expurgating content.[136] Extensive cuts were made to limit the sexual licentiousness in – and to excise the unmarried Julia's pregnancy from – the latter play, while references to the potential consummation of Othello and Desdemona's marriage were minimised in the former. As in *Titus*, then, *Measure* and *Othello* were subject to the significant censorship of sexual relationships, especially interracial ones. Though the Bowdlers' editions received a fair share of contemporary critique for the scale of their redactions, their popularity reflected and helped to solidify the association of Shakespeare with domestic respectability.

Alongside its explicitly racist language, sexual violence, and bodily mutilation, the presentation of *Titus* as extreme, transgressive, and even dangerous lies also in its threat to this image of a paternalistic Shakespeare.

[134] Molly Yarn, *Shakespeare's 'Lady Editors': A New History of the Shakespearean Text* (Cambridge: Cambridge University Press, 2022), 22.

[135] Thomas Bowdler, *The Family Shakespeare, in Ten Volumes*, 10 vols. Eds. Thomas and Henrietta Bowdler (London: Longman, 1818), vol.1, x.

[136] Adam H. Kitzes, 'The Hazards of Expurgation: Adapting *Measure for Measure* to the Bowdler *Family Shakespeare*', *Journal for Early Modern Cultural Studies* 13.2 (2013): 43–68, 46.

The play stages a nightmarish inversion of the imagined scene treasured by the Bowdlers and the Lambs, in which Shakespeare as literary classical author is used as a tool for male relatives to instruct young women in a family setting. *Titus* is the only work of Shakespeare's to feature a scene of family reading, but it is the mutilated Lavinia who informs her male family members of her rape by prompting a communal reading of Ovid's *Metamorphoses*. Indeed, Lavinia herself is interpreted as a threat to the comparative safety of the Andronici's domestic space when she frightens her nephew by chasing him onstage in an attempt to claim his copy of Ovid. Here, too, it is Lavinia who is noted for her proficiency in literary interpretation: she is 'deeper read' than Lucius and is compared with the exemplary Roman educator of her sons, Cornelia.[137] She exercises her comprehensive knowledge of the book and imparts a warped kind of moral instruction by revealing the circumstances of her rape to her male relatives via the text. Far from the kind of edifying instruction envisioned by the Bowdlers, this scene of female-led family reading facilitates the play's final scenes of cannibalism and slaughter.

Though this scene does not contain the spectacles of violence seen elsewhere in the play, it nonetheless presents one additional way that the play transgresses from the inherited expectations around a canonical Shakespeare. If the nineteenth century saw a turn towards the construction of Shakespeare as a cultural (and colonial) father figure, with influence over the moral education of young girls within their family, *Titus* exemplifies the transgressive potential of female-led instruction and literary interpretation. The education and outreach programmes of institutions like the RSC are tied to this historical legacy of Shakespeare's works being used to instruct and moralise. In this context, then, *Titus* presents a challenge on two fronts: in its proliferation of adult themes and graphic content, but also in its opposition to the broader paternalistic literary authority represented by Shakespeare and wielded by institutions that stage and disseminate his works.

---

[137] William Shakespeare, *Titus Andronicus*, ed. Alan Hughes (Cambridge: Cambridge University Press, 2006), 4.1.12; 33.

In the RSC broadcast, McIntyre and Adegbola engaged explicitly with the question of *Titus* presenting a threatening example of moral deviance. In her interview, McIntyre argued that the way in which the play 'set[s] up a white, male establishment against women, non-white people and foreigners ... seems to me to be alarming as a potential path that society could go down today'.[138] Here, then, the broadcast introduced to cinema audiences a more specific locus of the play's difficulty and (im)moral extremities: its modelling of state violence against minority groups. In another pre-recorded interview clip, Adegbola suggested that the play 'is about a ruling class that has lost touch with those over whom they rule'.[139] *Titus* demonstrates the harmful consequences, Adegbola says, of 'a woman who has been treated really, really appallingly by, um, a masculine society – ... I'm talking specifically about Tamora who was a queen'.[140] Though elsewhere Adegbola references Aaron using his 'new power ... to redress the imbalances that he's experienced throughout his life as a black man', his broader statement of the play's immorality is focussed on the Roman's treatment of Tamora.[141] As a result, Adegbola's interview clips demonstrate the breadth of subjects who face political violence in the play – both his own character whose treatment is explicitly marked by his race, and Tamora whose treatment is marked (in Adegbola's assessment) by her gender.

In a play fixated with the idea of Roman ethnic and political 'purity', the attention given by Adegbola and McIntyre to the problematic racial politics of *Titus* further emphasises its challenges for contemporary audiences. As Francesca T Royster highlights, *Titus* features more instances of the word 'hue' than any other Shakespearean work.[142] McIntyre's statement that the action of the play targets primarily 'women, non-white people and foreigners', resonates with Carol Mejia LaPerle's assessment that *Titus*

---

[138] [Pre-recorded Interview] RSC Live, *Titus Andronicus*.

[139] [Pre-show Short Film] RSC Live, *Titus Andronicus*.

[140] [Pre-show Short Film] RSC Live, *Titus Andronicus*.

[141] [Pre-show Short Film] RSC Live, *Titus Andronicus*.

[142] Francesca T. Royster, 'White-Limed Walls: Whiteness and Gothic Extremism in Shakespeare's *Titus Andronicus*', *Shakespeare Quarterly* 51.4 (2000): 432–455, 434.

'criminalizes the racialized subject's social agency'.[143] Adegbola's emphasis on Tamora as a principal victim reminds us that the Goth characters are also persistently presented as ethnically 'Other' – a strand of the play's racial dynamics which is frequently explored and emphasised through casting and costume choices in performance.[144] Royster likewise argues that attention to Tamora's paleness is crucial to the broader 'othering of a woman who is conspicuously white'.[145] Thus the 'striking fairness' of Tamora and her Goth sons is a further extension of the play's anxiety around the threat posed by miscegenation to the Roman state.[146] A part of the play's extremity, Adegbola and McIntyre's interview clips seemed to imply, might be its atypical preoccupation not only with violence, but with violence specifically against racialised groups.

McIntyre and Adegbola's interview clips were the first of the broadcast to engage with race in *Titus Andronicus*, and both establish a clear image of racial oppression at the heart of the play's extreme violence. As the broadcast developed, their set-up offered an opportunity to value *Titus* as a play with contemporary relevance and with a useful moral warning. McIntyre

---

[143] LaPerle, '"If I Might Have My Will"', 137.

[144] In McIntyre's production, the principal Goth characters were introduced in prison jumpsuits to emphasise their status as captives. Later, Nia Gwynne's Tamora was shown to largely assimilate with the designer fashions of the Roman political elite, wearing a quilted outdoor jacket similar to a Barbour jacket worn by Lavinia (Hannah Morrish) to the hunt in Act 2. However, hair styling was used to differentiate Goth characters from Romans in different ways: as Empress, Tamora retained three high buns which created a Mohican effect. Similarly, later in the production Amber James's Goth general wore long dreadlocks. The more punkish and natural hairstyles worn by Gwynne and James contrasted the highly feminised and manicured Lavinia, whose hair was arranged in 1940s-style victory rolls.

[145] Royster, 'White-Limed Walls', 433.

[146] Royster, 'White-Limed Walls', 433; the 'othering' of the Goth characters and the play's anxiety surrounding miscegenation is also the focus of David Sterling Brown's chapter, 'Somatic Similarity: The White Other and *Titus Andronicus*' in *Shakespeare's White Others* (Cambridge: Cambridge University Press, 2023), 36–60.

states in her interview that the play's structure of retributive violence is 'a good reason to watch *Titus Andronicus* just as a set of markers for what we should all of us not be doing'.[147] Similarly, Adegbola reflects that the performance should be 'a great opportunity to sit down for three hours and have a think about [the play] together as a community'.[148] If the image of a paternalistic and instructional Shakespeare operated behind some of this broadcast's positioning of *Titus* as a transgressive Shakespearean 'alternative', this framing of the play's racialised oppression offered a different kind of exemplar. This is, as McIntyre suggests, 'what we should all of us *not* be doing'.[149] As such, *Titus*'s portrayal of violence against the Othered Goth characters, and its presentation of an excessively stereotyped Black villain in Aaron, was assimilated into another image of an instructional Shakespeare.

There is evidence elsewhere in the paratextual history of *Titus* of a fraught relationship between violence and race, and between relevance and the play's landscape of catastrophic moral and political collapse. The danger that *Titus* might dramatise destructive moral exemplars – as classical precedents do for characters within the play – is a much-overlooked concern in Edward Ravenscroft's adaptation of the play, *Titus Andronicus, or, The Rape of Lavinia* (1687, hereafter *Lavinia* to distinguish from Shakespeare and Peele's play). A handful of lines from the preface to the printed play, which denounce *Titus* as 'rather a heap of Rubbish than a structure', are frequently cited as early evidence of a tradition of critical disapproval.[150] Ravenscroft's claim that the play 'was not Originally his [i.e., Shakespeare's]' and that he 'only gave some Master-touches to one or two of the Principal Parts or Characters' are similarly often quoted in discussions of the play's co-authorship.[151] Elsewhere the framing of Ravenscroft's edition shares a focus with the RSC's broadcast of *Titus* on the play's potential to offer a dangerous form of moral instruction.

---

[147] [Pre-recorded Interview] RSC Live, *Titus Andronicus*.

[148] [Pre-show Short Film] RSC Live, *Titus Andronicus*.

[149] [Pre-recorded Interview] RSC Live, *Titus Andronicus*, emphasis added.

[150] Edward Ravenscroft, *Titus Andronicus, or the Rape of Lavinia* (London: J. Hindmarsh, 1687), A2r.

[151] Ravenscroft, *Titus Andronicus, or the Rape of Lavinia*, A2r.

Performed in 1678 with apparently little success, Ravenscroft saw to print *Lavinia* nine years later. The prefatory materials to the print edition of the play comprises a title page, *dramatis personae*, dedicatory epistle, an address to the reader, together with an epilogue and three substituted prologues (the originals, Ravenscroft alleged, had been lost). A crucial context for the performance and printing of *Lavinia* is the Popish Plot: a period a feverish civic unrest and anti-Catholic riots spanning the period between 1678 and 1681. This widespread panic was fuelled largely by the 'discovery' by Titus Oates of a fictitious conspiracy to assassinate Charles II and place his Catholic brother, James II, on the throne. The epistle to *Lavinia* is addressed to Henry Arundell, 3rd Baron of Wardour, who had been imprisoned amid the false accusations of the Plot.[152] The unrest caused by the plot had been quelled and Oates, its principal instigator, imprisoned by the time Ravenscroft's play was published in 1687. Nonetheless, the political and social contexts of the play's first performances are continually referenced in the paratextual materials.

As in Adegbola and McIntyre's interviews, Ravenscroft's dedicatory epistle to Arundell is concerned with the corrupting potential of the moral example set by his alteration to the play in the context of late seventeenth-century social and political landscape. Critics have noted how Ravenscroft's changes amplify the violence of *Titus* instead of mitigating it: partly in line with his broader representation of Lavinia's rape as 'An Invasion on a Prince's Right' to parallel the anti-Catholic resistance to the proposed accession of James II.[153] Moreover, Ravenscroft's violent additions centre

---

[152] Peter Sherlock, 'Arundell, Henry, third Baron Arundell of Wardour (bap. 1608, d. 1694), royalist army officer and politician.' *Oxford Dictionary of National Biography*, Oxford University Press, www.oxforddnb.com/view/10.1093/ref:odnb/9780198614128.001.0001/odnb-9780198614128-e-716 [accessed 13 May 2023]

[153] Ravenscroft, *Titus Andronicus, or the Rape of Lavinia*, C4v. For the play's allusions to the Exclusion Crisis (1679–81), see Depledge, *Shakespeare's Rise*, 116; Hazelton Spencer, *Shakespeare Improved: The Restoration Versions in Quarto and on the Stage* (New York: Frederick Ungar, 1927), 287–292; and Barbara Burgess-Van Aken, 'Contexts of Fear: Edward Ravenscroft's

on creating a spectacle from the suffering of Black bodies more emphatically than in Shakespeare and Peele's version.[154] Ravenscroft adapted his source text to erase all the care Aaron takes to protect his and Tamora's child, instead incorporating the baby into a monstrous spectacle of voluntary cannibalism to mirror Tamora's involuntary consumption of her own sons.[155] After Tamora has killed their baby, Aaron asks her to relinquish the infant's body: 'She has out-done me in my own Art – / Out-done me in Murder – kill'd her own Child. / Give it me – I'le eat it.'[156] One of Ravenscroft's few original scenes, and what Ayanna Thompson argues to be his 'largest revision to *Titus*', stages Aaron being tortured on a rack and subsequently burnt alive by Titus.[157]

Ravenscroft's amplification of the play's violence forms a crucial subtext for the moralising tone of his epistle:

> In all sorts of Government Plays have been judg'd both Commendable and Profitable, Especially Tragedies, that by representing Hero's, Youth might be taught great Actions, and inspir'd with a Noble Courage to perform and imitate; and by Exposing Base and Ignoble deeds, divert and deter the ungenerous from their practices. This piece was Calculated to that Season, when Villainy, Treachery and

Adaptation of Shakespeare's *Titus Andronicus*', *Actes des Congres de la Societe Francaise Shakespeare* 36 (2018): 1–14.

[154] Ayanna Tene Thompson, 'Depicting Race and Torture on the Early Modern Stage' (Doctoral Thesis, Harvard University, 2001), 138–159.

[155] In Shakespeare and Peele's original, Aaron defends his child twice against threats to have him executed – in the first instance, against Chiron and Demetrius ('This maugre all the world will I keep safe / or some of you shall smoke for it in Rome', 4.2.11). Later in the play, Aaron is captured by Lucius and two Goths while attempting to transport the child to a Goth family for safety. Aaron's subsequent confession is prompted by Lucius's threat to kill his son (5.1.20-146). William Shakespeare, *Titus Andronicus*, ed. Alan Hughes (Cambridge: Cambridge University Press, 2006).

[156] Ravenscroft, *Titus Andronicus, or the Rape of Lavinia*, H4r.

[157] Thompson, 'Depicting Race and Torture', 155.

> Perjury, Triumph'd over Truth, Innocence and Loyalty. In
> some degree the End answer'd the Design, for it gaul'd the
> Plotting Factioun by shewing Actions so like their own, and
> had prov'd the Stages Martyr, had it not been supported and
> defended by the Loyal and the Brave.[158]

In this conceptualisation, the value of Ravenscroft's adaptation (and by extension, the play from which it was altered) was in acting as a litmus test for contemporary virtue: those who supported the play's initial performance did so because their consciences were clear of the very 'Villainy, Treachery, and Perjury' the play dramatises.[159]

Elsewhere in the prefatory paratexts to Ravenscroft's play, this altered *Titus* is framed as risking commercial failure due to the depravity of its characters and action. In an address to the reader, Ravenscroft reiterates his claim that he staged the work out of a sense of moral obligation, adding that he was 'content rather to lose the Profit, then not expose to the World the Picture of such Knaves and Rascals as then Reign'd in the opinion of the Foolish and Malicious part of the Nation'.[160] In effect, this framing of *Lavinia* reverses the same narrative of the play's relevance and value which McIntyre gives as part of the *Titus* broadcast: rather than a warning of 'potential paths that society could go down', Ravenscroft argues for the necessity of his alteration (in all its moral depravity) in helping to reshape the recent past.[161] In other words, audiences that do *not* heed the play's message might end up astray.

Read in conversation with this prefatory concern with civil disorder, Ravenscroft's amplification of state violence towards Aaron and his child depicts the play's racialised characters even more clearly as ciphers for the disruption and culture of fear stirred by the Popish Plot. Moreover, in a play which figures that same disorder as a kind of political rape, Aaron is assigned more implicit agency in Lavinia's rape than its actual perpetrators,

---

[158] Ravenscroft, *Titus Andronicus, or the Rape of Lavinia*, A1r–A1v.

[159] Ravenscroft, *Titus Andronicus, or the Rape of Lavinia*, A1v.

[160] Ravenscroft, *Titus Andronicus, or the Rape of Lavinia*, A2v.

[161] [Pre-recorded Interview] RSC Live, *Titus Andronicus*.

Chiron and Demetrius. As Ayanna Thompson notes, Ravenscroft's adaptation anticipates that audiences will 'revel in [Aaron's] racking and feel secure with his final burning, a visible purgation of Rome'.[162] The preface's feverish fixation on civil disorder – and how it was quelled in part by Ravenscroft's play – underscores the torture and consumption of the Black body as an act of political pacification and crucially situates it in a reader's contemporary political context. In this regard, it mirrors the kind of framing offered by McIntyre's interview for the RSC broadcast of *Titus*, in which the director argues for the relevance of the play by creating an implicit contemporary parallel with its violence of a 'white, male establishment against women, non-white people and foreigners'.[163] The play's political relevance in Ravenscroft's edition, as in the RSC's broadcast, is thus inherently but implicitly tied to its racial politics.[164]

Ravenscroft's alteration parallels the RSC's broadcast paratexts in one other significant way: its recognition of Shakespeare as an authorial presence. As I suggest previously, the RSC's *Titus* broadcast was emphatic in its sole attribution of the play to Shakespeare – perhaps in recognition that the violence and spectacle which had previously made the play distasteful to critics and editors can now be subsumed into an appealing shock value.[165] Closer attention to the framing of *Lavinia* in its different iterations likewise suggests how the authorial identity of the play is malleable in line with the value of relevance. The play was printed with three prologues and an epilogue to supplement the performed originals, which Ravenscroft claims were lost '[i]n the Hurry of those distracted times', that is, during the early period of the Plot.[166] The printed prologues resonate with the broader chastising of the Plot conspirators seen in the epistle and address, with commentary on the contemporary Exclusion Crisis and satire moralising against the idleness of politicians.

These political and satirical concerns mean that the three supplemented prologues are much less invested in Shakespeare's ownership of

---

[162] Thompson, 'Depicting Race and Torture', 155.

[163] [Pre-recorded Interview] RSC Live, *Titus Andronicus*.

[164] Depledge, *Shakespeare's Rise*, 70. [165] Karim-Cooper, 'Introduction', 1–3.

[166] Ravenscroft, *Titus Andronicus, or the Rape of Lavinia*, A2v.

the source text than is the surviving section of *Lavinia*'s prologue for the stage. Partly retained in Gerard Laingbaine's *An Account of the English Dramatick Poets* (1691), the eight-line extract emphasises the Shakespearean credentials of Ravenscroft's source text and may have even been spoken by the figure of Shakespeare himself: '*Shakespeare* by him [Ravenscroft] reviv'd now treads the Stage.'[167] In this prologue, it is Shakespeare's association with the Ravenscroft's source text which confirms the value of the alteration, as Ravenscroft rests comfortably '[u]nder his [Shakespeare's] sacred Lawrels ... / Safe from the blast of any Criticks Frown'.[168]

By comparison, Ravenscroft's later print paratexts demonstrate a markedly different approach to Shakespearean authorship of *Titus*. In his address to the reader, Ravenscroft's assessment of the play's demerits is such that he is 'apt to believe' the report that Shakespeare's own work in *Titus* is limited to 'some Master-touches' and that the play is 'not Originally his'.[169] Read in conversation with the replaced prologues, the print edition of Ravenscroft's *Titus* is decidedly more interested in the value of the altered play as a commentary on the recent politics of the Popish Plot than they are in calling upon Shakespeare as a validating authorial figure. Similarly, where the original prologue minimises the scale of Ravenscroft's alterations (the playwright 'but winnow'd *Shakespear*'s Corn'), the printed Address boasts that if readers were to '[c]ompare the Old Play with this, you'll finde that none in all that Authors Works ever received greater Alterations or Additions'.[170] Emma Depledge summarises the distinctions between these two versions of Ravenscroft retelling his adaptations, noting that '[t]he theatrical paratexts stressed sameness and moderate alteration, but the

---

[167] Gerard Laingbane, *An Account of the English Dramatick Poets, or, Some Observations and Remarks on the Lives and Writings of All Those that Have Publish'd either Comedies, Tragedies, Tragi-Comedies, Pastorals, Masques, Interludes, Farces or Opera's in the English Tongue* (Oxford: George West and Henry Clements, 1691), Ggr.

[168] Laingbane, *An Account of the English Dramatick Poets*, Ggr.

[169] Ravenscroft, *Titus Andronicus, or the Rape of Lavinia*, A2r.

[170] Ravenscroft, *Titus Andronicus, or the Rape of Lavinia*, A2v.

readerly paratexts ... instead emphasized novelty, originality, and political loyalties'.[171]

This balance between familiarity and radical difference remained instrumental to the framing of *Titus* for the contemporary audiences to the RSC's live broadcast. While marking the play as excessive, disturbing, and deeply transgressive, paratexts to this broadcast nonetheless called upon a roster of tried and tested narratives of Shakespearean value. The play is still, this broadcast seemed anxious to establish, authorially Shakespearean (to the extent of excluding Peele); morally instructive; and politically relevant.

Moreover, while these narratives of value have varied significantly in the play's critical and editorial history, the paratexts to Ravenscroft's adaptation remind us that their incorporation into new iterations of the play in print and performance have deep roots. The play's broader adaptation and print history helps to elucidate the ways in which the reputation of *Titus* is being rehabilitated for contemporary audiences along lines of relevance, as well as capitalising on the play's extremes of violence. Yet the critical and performance turn for the play is, as the RSC's broadcast suggests, dependent on its being able to push against the limits of what a 'Shakespeare' play can be. If the framing of *Titus* for contemporary audiences invests in the value of the alt-Shakespearean – the transgressive alternative which nonetheless is firmly granted canonical security – then we ought to question how effective the play can be at challenging narratives of Shakespearean cultural value from that position inside the canon.

Is *Titus* really able to 'jolt Shakespearean performance out of a perceived conservative malaise', as productions of not-Shakespeare often seek to do?[172] The framing of the play in the RSC's broadcast embraced its difference to the extent that *Titus* was able to function as a refreshing rebel within the canon, but not to the extent that the play's troubling racial or sexual politics formed a significant part of that alterity. In this respect, too, the play's print and adaptation history is instructive. As in the Bowdlers' editions and in Ravenscroft's adaptation, *Titus* remains subject to processes of censorship, alteration, and oversimplification in order for it to be comfortably subsumed into new Shakespearean canonising projects.

[171] Depledge, *Shakespeare's Rise*, 144. [172] Price, 'Canon', 152.

3 Fictions of Composition: *The Merry Wives of Windsor* (2018)

In the first collected edition of Shakespeare's works published in the eighteenth century, the poet and dramatist Nicholas Rowe offers a tentative reflection on the relationship between Shakespeare's life and his works: 'Tho' the Works of Mr. *Shakespear* may seem to many not to want a Comment, yet I fancy some little Account of the Man himself may not be thought improper to go along with them.'[173] Rowe's prefacing *Account of the Life, &c. of Mr. William Shakespear* was included in the first volume of his six-octavo edition of the plays (1709). In his statement that Shakespeare's works do not need a biographical gloss, Rowe makes an implicit suggestion that the worth of the plays exists independently from general interest in the life of their author. Yet some plays are frequently attached to, and explained through, imagined versions of Shakespeare's life and working practice – including, for example, the associations of a young (and reckless?) Shakespeare we have seen tethered to *The Two Gentlemen of Verona* and *Titus Andronicus*. However, no play is more closely associated with an image of Shakespeare's working practice and artistic conditions than *The Merry Wives of Windsor*.

This section is concerned with the intersections of biography and artistic practice, and how both were used to explain and excuse the perceived deficiencies of *Merry Wives* in the RSC's 2018 broadcast of the play. The broadcast featured a live interview between Suzy Klein and the production's stage director, Fiona Laird. The foremost subject of discussion in the interview was the apocryphal theory that *Merry Wives* was commissioned by Queen Elizabeth I and, as Klein and Laird suggested, that this was a particularly hasty commission. Laird stated her impression that the play was 'obviously written very quickly'.[174] This statement and the interview more generally was crucially underpinned by a value judgement of the play as

---

[173] Nicholas Rowe, 'Some Account of the Life &c. of Mr. *William Shakespeare*', in *The Works of Mr. William Shakespear; in Six Volumes*, 6 vols., ed. Nicholas Rowe (London: Jacob Tonson, 1709), I: a1v.

[174] [Live Interview] RSC Live, *The Merry Wives of Windsor*, directed for the screen by Dewi Humphreys, Royal Shakespeare Theatre, Stratford-upon-Avon (12 September 2018).

somehow artistically deficient. Moreover, in Laird's suggestion that a rushed composition is 'obvious', we see the recurrence once more of an implicit, elevated artistic standard for Shakespeare's works against which this play was positioned. *Merry Wives* was, in this paratextual framing, a work in desperate need of the kind of semi-biographical gloss which Rowe denounced as superfluous. To understand how the theory of royal commission operated in relation to the artistic merits of *Merry Wives* in this broadcast, I draw on two print paratexts that indulge in the same biographical fantasy of a Shakespeare-Elizabeth interaction. These are Rowe's own *Account*, and, published seven years earlier, the preface to John Dennis's adaptation of *Merry Wives*, titled *The Comical Gallant: or, The Amours of Sir John Falstaffe* (1702).[175]

I consider how the RSC's broadcast draws on a long tradition of (de) valuing the play through this pseudo-biographical anecdote, as well as the implications of this myth for prevailing ideas about Shakespeare's artistic exceptionalism. In a broader narrative of Shakespeare's most accomplished works being composed in a state of solitary genius, *Merry Wives* is a paradox which both threatens and appeals. On the one hand, the play's apparent deficiency threatens assumptions of Shakespeare's elevated cultural value and yet also presents the opportunity for a tantalising exchange between the two icons of early modern England. Such is the commercial appeal of a Shakespeare-Elizabeth interaction that it did not simply form a focus of the paratextual framing of the RSC's broadcast – it was instead integral to the 'text' of the production itself.

Laird's production featured an interpolated prologue scene, which imagined the composition of *Merry Wives*. In this prefatory stage action, a messenger was heard arriving at Shakespeare's lodgings to deliver a letter. An actor playing Shakespeare was shown only in silhouette, while the content of the letter was read by an animated portrait of Elizabeth I, projected onto a screen onstage. Elizabeth's letter self-consciously developed

[175] John Dennis, *The Comical Gallant: or, the Amours of Sir John Falstaffe: A Comedy, as It Is Acted at the Theatre Royal in Drury-Lane. By his Majestie's Servants. By Mr Dennis. To which is added, A large Account of the Taste in Poetry, and the Causes of the Degeneracy of It* (London: A. Baldwin, 1702).

a number of elements behind the commission myth, including showing the Queen stating that her 'admiration for [Shakespeare's] work for the stage is well known', and that the motive behind her request is her preference for 'that excellent rogue Sir John Falstaffe'.[176] It is Elizabeth's request that the 'new play' be completed with a fortnight which elicits the first reaction from Shakespeare, who interjects with 'Oh my God!'[177] Shakespeare's audible panic was substantiated at the end of this sequence, when the playwright was seen beginning to furiously scrawl the script of *Merry Wives*.

The theatre production, then, was structured to clearly foreground the theory that the play was written as a last-minute commission for the Queen and to emphasise a sense of Shakespeare working in a frantic heat of composition. However, cinema audiences received an additional version of this commission myth before the start of the production, one which was much more explicitly tied to a negative assessment of the value of the play. This came primarily in the form of the live interview between Klein and Laird, in which the latter forwarded the theory that the play was written 'in about two weeks'.[178] Laird connected this haste to the play's assumed demerits:

> Laird: We can't get Shakespeare on the phone and ask him exactly, but we can piece together – I think it was written to commission. It was obviously written very quickly [...] I think he actually did the 1599 equivalent of calling his friend who did the funny French accent and his friend who did the funny Welsh accent and [...] put it together as a royal entertainment really quickly.
>
> Klein: A very scrappily put together thing, then.[179]

This narrative of the play's composition relies on a judgement that remains largely unspecified. The sense that the play is 'scrappily put together' might

---

[176] *The Merry Wives of Windsor* directed by Fiona Laird. The Royal Shakespeare Theatre, Stratford-upon-Avon.

[177] *The Merry Wives of Windsor*, directed by Fiona Laird.

[178] [Live Interview] RSC Live, *The Merry Wives of Windsor*.

[179] [Live Interview] RSC Live, *The Merry Wives of Windsor*.

allude to the fact that *Merry Wives* exists in two early texts: a 1602 Quarto which is distinctly more streamlined that the version printed in the First Folio of 1623.[180] There has been considerable debate as to whether the Quarto *Merry Wives* is a memorial reconstruction (most likely by the actor in the role of Host of the Garter), or whether this earlier text represents a revision of its later iteration in the Folio.[181] With this complex textual history, and with two distinct early textual witnesses of the play to draw from, there was ample scope for Klein and Laird to discuss the challenges of editing and adapting these two versions for performance. These early textual variants may have offered grounds for a discussion of the play as 'scrappily put together'.[182] Nonetheless, Laird's suggestion that the play was 'obviously written very quickly' is grounded not in these early variant texts, but in what she suggests in Shakespeare's overreliance on the accent capabilities of his fellow actors.[183]

Laird's description alludes to the 'clownishly exaggerated' figures of Dr Caius and Sir Hugh Evans, two foreigners who inhabit the otherwise parochial Windsor and represent parody French and Welsh stereotypes.[184] Tying these characters implicitly to the theory of a rushed commission suggests an anxiety about the play's caricaturing of language and identity. In this regard, the commission theory was used in this live interview as a way to pre-emptively excuse the systems of social inclusion and exclusion that proliferate throughout *Merry Wives*, a play deeply interested in what it means to be integrated as an outsider into a small community. That is to say that an anxiety over the reception of foreign characters was not simply a feature of this paratext but an inheritance from within the play itself. Underlying the negotiation of the play's problematic value within

[180] [Live Interview] RSC Live, *The Merry Wives of Windsor*.
[181] See Laurie Maguire and Emma Smith, 'Theater, Revision, and *The Merry Wives of Windsor*', *Shakespeare Quarterly* 72.3–4 (2022): 177–202.
[182] [Live Interview] RSC Live, *The Merry Wives of Windsor*.
[183] [Live Interview] RSC Live, *The Merry Wives of Windsor*.
[184] Patricia Akhimie, 'Racist Humour and Shakespearean Comedy', *The Cambridge Companion to Shakespeare and Race*, ed. Ayanna Thompson (Cambridge: Cambridge University Press, 2021), 47–61, 57.

Shakespeare's canon in this exchange is concern over what Patricia Akhimie has identified as 'the racist heuristic upon which Shakespeare's comedies capitalize and frequently rely'.[185] Despite Akhimie's observation that this reduction of character to 'type' is a common feature of Shakespeare's comedies, Laird and Klein's interview figured it as a kind of aberration for the playwright. This aberration, they suggested, is a consequence of the play as a rushed royal commission.

There may also be an underlying anxiety about genre at work in Laird's value judgement of the play. *Merry Wives*, as Callan Davies has observed, 'stands in contrast to some of those more regularly staged [i.e., Shakespearean comedies], such as *A Midsummer Night's Dream* and *As You Like It*, in its thematic concern with the kitchen sink'.[186] The play has a marked tone of 'citizen comedy' which, like the attention to moral depravity and violent excess I discuss in the previous section, is often more readily associated with the works of Shakespeare's contemporaries than with those by Shakespeare himself.[187] The generic tone and domestic concerns of *Merry Wives*, like its parodic representations of non-English characters, is disconcertingly unfamiliar when compared with many of Shakespeare's more canonically central comedies.

By suggesting that the responsibility for the play's demerits rested on outside creative agents and artistic restraints, this broadcast also rehearsed familiar narratives of Shakespeare's cultural value and working practices. There is a long-standing association of Shakespeare's most canonically central and celebrated plays not only with sole authorship but also with a kind of untethered creative freedom and agency. As Emma Smith notes, 'The inspired poet model tends to produce tidy texts emphasizing linguistic fluency and singular authorship; the theatrical model is more interested in

---

[185] Akhimie, 'Racist Humour', 57.

[186] Callan Davies, introduction to William Shakespeare, *The Merry Wives of Windsor*, ed. Sarah Neville, The New Oxford Shakespeare (Oxford: Oxford University Press, 2024), 1–44, 1.

[187] David Crane, introduction to William Shakespeare, *The Merry Wives of Windsor*, 2nd ed., ed. David Crane (Cambridge: Cambridge University Press, 2010), 1–36, 6.

the idea that Shakespeare worked with other writers and that his works were themselves dynamic scripts rather than static literary monuments.'[188] These models have, historically, operated within a value hierarchy which prizes the isolated genius above the working theatrical collaborator. Indeed, the previous section considered how the emergent appeal of *Titus Andronicus* was linked to the broadcast's evasion of that play's co-authorship with George Peele. Similarly, Samuel Johnson's judgement that *Two Gentlemen* had escaped the 'the hazards of transcription' relies upon the implicit agreement between editor and reader that external creative agents – from actors to compositors and printers – were liable to muddy Shakespeare's clean 'originals'.[189] Laird's image of a Shakespeare 'calling his friend[s]' in order to 'put it [i.e., *Merry Wives*] together really quickly' constructs artistic collaboration as a last resort, rather than a potentially productive creative choice or, indeed, a regular and established practice of early modern theatre companies.[190] These are the 'contingencies of human production' in the period which, as Will Sharpe notes, Shakespeare is so often imagined as transcending.[191] The social purity of Windsor, articulated within the play in the contention to find a suitable husband for Anne Page, finds a parallel here in the way this broadcast established an implicit mistrust of the types of 'outside' collaboration that was commonplace in Shakespeare's working environment.

Of course, the other external influence implicated in Laird and Klein's iteration of the theory of *Merry Wives* as a royal commission is Elizabeth herself. In terms of mediating the value of *Merry Wives*, Elizabeth has a contingent but significant role in both the RSC's broadcast iteration and in historical print examples. While Elizabeth was only alluded to in the live interview through Laird's reference to a '*royal* entertainment', the later prologue interpolated into the stage production suggested Elizabeth's

---

[188] Emma Smith, preface to William Shakespeare, *The Merry Wives of Windsor*, ed. Sarah Neville, The New Oxford Shakespeare (Oxford: Oxford University Press, 2024), v–vi.

[189] Johnson, vol.1, 180n1.

[190] [Live Interview] RSC Live, *The Merry Wives of Windsor*.

[191] Sharpe, *Shakespeare and Collaborative Writing*, 2.

approval of his works.[192] In this regard, the RSC's live interview and performance prologue participate in a much broader tradition of the commission theory – and Elizabeth in particular – being used to negotiate a double-edged judgement of the merits of *Merry Wives*.

The earliest sustained suggestion that the play was commissioned by Elizabeth on two weeks' notice appears in John Dennis's 1702 adaptation, *The Comical Gallant: or, The Amours of Sir John Falstaffe* (hereafter *Gallant*). Dennis establishes the theory of a hasty royal commission in two paratexts to the print edition of his play: an epistle and a prologue. The reference to the supposed commission first appears in the epistle, which is addressed to the Tory politician and Dennis's fellow playwright, George Granville. This narrative of the play's provenance is, as in the RSC's broadcast, deeply tied to a judgement of its value:

> When I first communicated the design which I had of altering this Comedy of *Shakespear*, I found that I should have two sorts of People to deal with, who would equally endeavour to obstruct my success. The one believed it to be so admirable, that nothing ought to be added to it; the other fancied it to be so despicable, that any ones time would be lost upon it.[193]

It is thus against the charge that *Merry Wives* is 'so despicable' that Dennis introduces his iteration of the commission theory. In this respect, Dennis's epistle shares with Klein and Laird's interview the anticipation that at least some of his audience will have a pre-existing negative judgement of *Merry Wives*.

Against these judgements of the play's deficiency, Elizabeth's approval of the play via the theory of royal commission allows Dennis to call upon an established historical authority to justify the exercise of adapting *Merry Wives*. Elizabeth is first among three authorities which Dennis lists to support his view that the play was worthy of his time. 'I knew very well,'

---

[192] [Live Interview] RSC Live, *The Merry Wives of Windsor*.
[193] Dennis, *The Comical Gallant*, A2r.

Dennis suggests, 'that [*Merry Wives*] had pleas'd one of the greatest Queens that ever was in the World.'[194] The second authority for the merit of the play is found in its recent performance history, as Dennis notes it was popular on the stage during the reign of Charles II, 'when People had an admirable taste of Comedy'.[195] Finally, Dennis trusts to his own judgement, qualified as it is by 'so long an acquaintance . . . with the best Comick Poets, among the Antients and Moderns'.[196] It is significant that the commission theory appears first in Dennis's epistle in order to defend and qualify the value of *Merry Wives*, rather than in the RSC's broadcast to excuse its deficiency against an assumed standard of Shakespeare's broader works. For the purposes of justifying his own adaptation, the provenance of *Merry Wives* is a way of explaining a positive value judgement of the play, not of excusing a negative one.

It is also telling that in Dennis's epistle, held against the prevailing standards of Augustan neoclassicism, Elizabeth is *one* among a *group* of authorities which includes Dennis himself. By comparison, she is the sole justification for Shakespeare's artistic ability in the RSC's interpolated prologue sequence. Especially following from the interview between Laird and Klein which implicitly disparaged the play, the sequence in which the projected portrait version of Elizabeth expresses her 'admiration for his [i.e., Shakespeare's] work' allows Elizabeth to stand as the primary champion and defendant of Shakespeare.[197] The context for the RSC's reiteration of the commission theory is crucial for its role in framing the value of the play, then. For Dennis, writing in a century that would see the development of Shakespeare's artistic exceptionalism, a greater number of defenders are called upon to qualify the value of the play. Its value is not nearly as assumed as in a broadcast production by the *Royal Shakespeare* Company, whose name not only signals the artistic elevation of this single playwright but grants him the cultural significance of monarchical association (and, by implication, the approval of successive monarchs long after his own Queen Elizabeth).

---

[194] Dennis, *The Comical Gallant*, A2r. [195] Dennis, *The Comical Gallant*, A2r.
[196] Dennis, *The Comical Gallant*, A2r.
[197] *The Merry Wives of Windsor*, directed by Fiona Laird.

Though it is clear that Elizabeth is the source of the royal commission to Shakespeare, Dennis's epistle and later Prologue are coy about naming the monarch directly. The Prologue features only allusions to a 'Comick Muse' and 'her Sprightly Train' being the source of Shakespeare's inspiration.[198] However, nowhere in his multiple references to royal commission in the epistle does Dennis name Elizabeth outright. References to Elizabeth appear instead under ciphers which emphasise her royal status, her active patronage of the arts, and her discerning taste in drama. This ambiguity suggests that implicit in Dennis's development of the commission theory are his own commercial concerns. The early eighteenth century was a particularly challenging period for the adaptation and commission of new plays, and Dennis's own epistle recalls how *Gallant* was a failure on the stage. As Katherine West Scheil has highlighted, this was a period which was not characterised by an active royal patronage of the arts under Queen Anne, crowned in the same year as the printing of *Gallant*.[199] Conjuring Elizabeth by her status and artistic discernment rather than by name, then, Dennis may have hoped to frame the theory of *Merry Wives* as a commission piece in such a way as to also act as a plea for greater royal patronage from his own newly crowned Queen.

As was seen in Ravenscroft's epistle to Arundell, too, Dennis's choice of George Granville as his addressee is relevant to how he uses the commission theory to frame the value of *Merry Wives* and of *Gallant*. Granville's own adaptation of *The Merchant of Venice* as *The Jew of Venice* (1701) was a rare success in a theatrical culture whose taste for comic entertainment was turning decidedly towards acrobatic spectacle and continental Opera.[200] Dennis's decision to conjure Elizabeth through her status and her taste may have been a prudent tactic to inspire a similar spirit of generosity in Granville. As such, Dennis might have hoped to use the negotiation of

---

[198] Dennis, *The Comical Gallant*, H1v.

[199] Katherine West Scheil, *The Taste of the Town: Shakespearian Comedy and the Early Eighteenth Century Theater* (London: Associated University Presses, 2003), 87.

[200] Scheil, *The Taste of the Town*, 98 and 135; and Michael Dobson, *The Making of the National Poet*, 125.

Merry Wives' complex value – and Elizabeth's endorsement of that value – to generate real financial capital in aid of his struggling theatrical ambitions.

When and how Elizabeth is named in relation to the play is thus intricately linked to the value judgements that the commission theory can be used to support. In the RSC's broadcast, for example, the initial establishment of the theory of hasty royal commission that Klein and Laird presented in their interview also did not name Elizabeth. However, when addressing a question from Klein about the production's costume and design choices, Laird emphasised that 'the beating heart of this play is Elizabethan – its Elizabethan language, it was written in the Elizabethan era'.[201] This discussion of the play's style and quality then turned towards a markedly more defensive consideration of its relevance. 'You can't take that away from' *Merry Wives*, Laird continued, 'you can't pretend like it was written last week because it wasn't. So, we have to keep that beating heart alive but make it recognisable to a contemporary Elizabethan audience'.[202]

Despite Elizabeth being an unnamed presence in her earlier discussion of the play's composition, Laird's statement about the characteristically 'Elizabethan' quality of *Merry Wives* created a saturation of the monarch's name (which was, as Laird alludes to, also the name of England's reigning monarch at the time of this broadcast). The emphasis on the play as unavoidably and irrevocably Elizabethan suggests that the challenge of *Merry Wives* is that it is almost *too* rooted in its historical period. By implication, *Merry Wives* suffers from a lack of the timeless and adaptable quality often associated with Shakespeare's works. Continually describing the play as definitively 'Elizabethan' may have registered with cinema audiences as a more antiquarian judgement than is typically forwarded for Shakespeare's works in live theatre broadcasts (and, indeed, in theatrical paratexts), where framing often devotes considerable attention to arguing a play's contemporary relevance. Assertions of the relevance of *Titus* were seen in the previous section, for example, while the 'run-through' style dynamism used to frame *Two Gentlemen* suggests that the play is too unfixed to be confined to a particular historical context. In this regard, Laird's

---

[201] [Live Interview] RSC Live, *The Merry Wives of Windsor*.
[202] [Live Interview] RSC Live, *The Merry Wives of Windsor*.

comment that a director has to 'keep that beating heart alive' sounds anxiously literal – as if the play, like Dennis's adaptation, risks flatlining when presented to audiences removed from its original context.[203]

Dennis is similarly concerned to frame his adaptation of *Merry Wives* with an eye to the difficulty of presenting the play to contemporary audiences. His telling of the commission narrative exists within a broader critique of theatrical tastes, and the epistle is advertised, on *Gallant*'s title page, as 'A large Account of the Taste in Poetry, and the Causes of the Degeneracy of it'.[204] Dennis gestures towards the prevailing taste for Aristotelian unities of action, arguing that the 'strange Defects' of *Merry Wives* have become stranger and 'less endured as the Stage growes more Regular'.[205] We might see this as a parallel to Laird's insistence on the play's Elizabethan-ness, which hints at the challenges of staging the *Merry Wives* for contemporary audiences without outright labelling the play as outdated or archaic. Dennis uses a comparable tactic in his claim that the play suffers from the development of different dramatic tastes, partially absolving Shakespeare himself while forwarding a negative judgement of his play. Like Laird's inescapably 'Elizabethan' Shakespeare, the Shakespeare of Dennis's epistle is only guilty of dying a century before the prevailing taste for 'Regular' drama.

The epistle and Prologue to *Gallant* are also interested in how the haste of the commission theory can be used to explain some of the deficiencies of *Merry Wives*. Dennis's paratexts, like Laird's assessment that the play was '*obviously* written very quickly' and had to be 'put ... together' at short notice, emphasise a sense of excusal when reiterating this element of the play's reputed composition.[206] Dennis is credited as having introduced the timescale of fourteen days to the theory that the play was commissioned by Elizabeth, perhaps developing the hint on the quarto title page that the play has been performed 'before her Majestie, and else-where'.[207] Dennis

[203] [Live Interview] RSC Live, *The Merry Wives of Windsor*.
[204] Dennis, *The Comical Gallant*, A1r. [205] Dennis, *The Comical Gallant*, A2v.
[206] [Live Interview] RSC Live, *The Merry Wives of Windsor*.
[207] William Shakespeare, *A Most Pleasant and Excellent Conceited Comedie, of Syr John Falstaffe, and the Merrie Wives of Windsor* (London: Arthur Johnson, 1602), A1r.

reiterates the exigency of the commission throughout his epistle, stating that Elizabeth was 'so eager to see the play [i.e., *Merry Wives*] Acted, that she commanded it to be finished in fourteen days'.[208] He uses this to further qualify his decision to adapt the play when he argues that 'in so short a time as this Play was writ, nothing could be done that is perfect'.[209] In a later critique of the style of *Merry Wives* in the epistle, Dennis returns again to 'fourteen days' given for the play's composition: 'This is not said in the least with a design to derogate from Shakespeare's merit, who performed more than anyone else could have done in so short a time.'[210] The basis for Dennis's critique of *Merry Wives*, then, continually absolves Shakespeare of individual responsibility for the challenge of creating the play within a fortnight.

Dennis's Prologue to *Gallant* develops the theme of haste in a similar way and offers a particularly illustrative comparison to the interpolated prologue of the RSC's production. The prologue doubles down on a paradoxical defence and critique of Shakespeare, returning to the limitations of a hasty composition:

> But Shakespeare's Play in fourteen days was writ,
> And in that space to make all just and fit
> Was an attempt surpassing human wit
> Yet our great *Shakespear*'s matchless Muse was such,
> None e're in so small time perform'd so much.[211]

As Adam H. Kitzes has observed, this image of Shakespeare writing in haste is one consistent with Dennis's broader critical reflections on the playwright.[212] In his *Essay on the Genius and Writings of Shakespear* (1712), Dennis notes that it may be 'easy to judge what time he was Master of, between his laborious Employment of Acting, and his continual Hurry of

---

[208] Dennis, *The Comical Gallant*, A2r. [209] Dennis, *The Comical Gallant*, A2v.

[210] Dennis, *The Comical Gallant*, A2v. [211] Dennis, *The Comical Gallant*, H1v.

[212] Adam H. Kitzes, 'John Dennis and the Shakespeare-Elizabeth Anecdote: *The Comical Gallant* and the Reception of *The Merry Wives of Windsor*', *Restoration and 18th Century Theatre Research* 28.2 (2013): 45–70.

Writing'.[213] In a similar imagined version of Shakespeare at work, Dennis's *Essay* claims that the playwright 'was perpetually call'd upon, by those who had the direction and Management of the Company to which he belong'd, for new Pieces'.[214] Here as in the RSC's broadcast, Shakespeare's abilities are imagined as contesting against the influence of external agents. However, the image of the playwright at work in Dennis's version is not tied to a particular value judgement. The association of collaboration and commercial limitations with Shakespeare's perceived weaker works, which was called upon implicitly in the RSC's *Merry Wives* broadcast, was still beginning to emerge at the time of Dennis's *Essay*.

Both Dennis's paratexts to *Gallant* and the RSC's broadcast paratexts invoke a complex relationship between the value of Shakespeare's works and the desire to substantiate aspects of the playwright's life. Imagining *Merry Wives* as a piece commissioned by Queen Elizabeth allows claims to be made about how Shakespeare might have interacted with other iconic figures of his lifetime as well as, crucially, the way(s) in which he composed his plays. What also unites these two paratextual examples is their suggestion that the play itself might be sufficient evidence to substantiate the theory of royal commission. The broadcast's paratextual features, including Laird and Klein's interview, failed to mention any early textual witnesses for the commission theory, including the play's 1602 quarto title page, Dennis's prefaces to *Gallant*, and its later mention in Rowe's edition of 1709. Laird's approach to evidencing the play's provenance depends entirely upon the same negative value judgement she proposed and which Klein echoed in her assessment of the play as a 'scrappily put together thing'.[215]

It is not always *exclusively* the value of *Merry Wives* that is being negotiated in paratextual discussions of the commission theory. As I have suggested in relation to the RSC's broadcast, this provenance narrative for the play was told selectively to reflect different strands of broader

---

[213] John Dennis, *An Essay on the Genius and Writings of Shakespear: With Some Letters of Criticism to the Spectator* (London: Bernard Lintott, 1712), C8v.

[214] Dennis, *An Essay on the Genius and Writings of Shakespear*, C8v.

[215] [Live Interview] RSC Live, *The Merry Wives of Windsor*.

Shakespearean value: the association of his greatest works with artistic and creative freedom, and the fantasy of his interacting with Queen Elizabeth I. In Rowe's *Account of the Life*, with which this section began, the theory of *Merry Wives* as a royal commission is turned towards a particularly ambiguous value judgement of the play itself. Rather, Rowe's rehearsal of this provenance narrative is used to establish an important and long-standing preoccupation with the value of Shakespeare himself as a biographical subject.

Rowe's *Account*, included as a preface to his collected edition of Shakespeare's works in 1709, was compiled with the assistance of the actor Thomas Betterton. Rowe and Betterton's reliance on hearsay and tradition would come to be thoroughly overshadowed by the considerably more comprehensive documentary efforts of Edmond Malone at the end of the century.[216] Margareta de Grazia has observed that the largely unsubstantiated anecdotes which make up Rowe's *Account* are organised not chronologically, but 'in the order of the social rank of persons Shakespeare encounters'.[217] Compelling narrative vignettes and snapshots – Shakespearean gossip – are priorities more discernible in the *Account* than the attempt to construct an ordered biographical timeline.

The *Account* appears anxious to establish a biographical presence for Shakespeare by yoking him with prominent named figures of the period. The commission myth thus becomes the most elevated in a series of narrative episodes through which Shakespeare's life acquires biographical evidence by association – typically with figures whose lives and activities are more substantially documented. Rowe's retelling of the commission theory is situated in a broader assertion that 'Queen *Elizabeth* had several of his Plays Acted before her, and without doubt gave him many gracious Marks of her Favour'.[218] According to Rowe, Elizabeth 'was so well pleas'd with that admirable Character of *Falstaff*, in the two Parts of Henry the Fourth, that she commanded

---

[216] Samuel Schoenbaum, *Shakespeare's Lives*, 2nd ed. (Oxford: Clarendon Press, 1991), 87; 178.

[217] Margareta de Grazia, *Shakespeare without a Life* (Oxford: Oxford University Press, 2023), 18.

[218] Rowe, *Account*, vol.1, a4v.

him [Shakespeare] to continue it for one Play more'.[219] The *Account* omits the deadline of a fortnight introduced by Dennis, and now includes a direction from Elizabeth that the play must 'shew' Falstaff 'in Love'.[220]

Margreta de Grazia has also argued that the anecdotes included within Rowe's *Account* effect their own implicit value judgements about Shakespeare's character. They encourage, de Grazia suggests, early eighteenth-century readers to align the contemporary ideas of Shakespeare's works as 'wild' and 'disordered' with episodes which evidence these qualities in his behaviour.[221] Indeed, this early example of a Shakespearean biography is one which continually shows the playwright 'breaking the laws of the land or overstepping the bounds of civility'.[222] When attached closely to a performance or adaptation of *Merry Wives*, the theory of Elizabeth's commission is often used to mitigate a supposed artistic transgression of Shakespeare's. However, in the context of Rowe's *Account*, implicit judgements of worth are more decidedly directed towards the character of Shakespeare himself. Rowe suggests that for readers to see 'how well it [i.e., Elizabeth's commission] was obey'd, the Play it self is an admirable Proof'.[223] This is, on the one hand, far from the suggestion made by both Dennis and the RSC's broadcast that the hasty composition of *Merry Wives* is a principal cause of its deficiency. Rather, this statement suggests a more ambiguous value judgement from Rowe – or, rather, it shows Rowe to pass on the making of that judgement to his readers. Is the play 'admirable Proof' of Shakespeare's artistic merits, or simply of his ability to follow the particular demands of Elizabeth's commission and 'shew [Falstaff] in Love'?[224] If the former, Rowe does not devote space in his *Account* to develop and argue for the merits of the play itself. If the latter is true, the play is 'admirable Proof' not of Shakespeare's genius but of his ability to follow orders.[225]

Rowe's edition thus fossilises an important moment in Shakespeare's textual history. Here, the beginning stages of a recognisable editorial

---

[219] Rowe, *Account*, vol.1, a4v–a5r. [220] Rowe, *Account*, vol.1, a5r.

[221] de Grazia, *Shakespeare without a Life*, 3.

[222] de Grazia, *Shakespeare without a Life*, 4. [223] Rowe, *Account*, vol.1, a5r

[224] Rowe, *Account*, vol.1, a5r [225] Rowe, *Account*, vol.1, a5r

tradition coincide with an expanded interest in the playwright's life. De Grazia and Brian Cummings have each considered the ways in which the concept of a 'biography' is alien to Rowe's *Account* – nonetheless, its anecdotal and often poorly substantiated details were repeatedly published alongside subsequent editions throughout the eighteenth century.[226] Shakespeare's canonisation in the period is thus intrinsically yoked to what is less a coherent biography than, as de Grazia puts it, a 'scattering of undated episodic incidents'.[227] That anecdotal quality is arguably still evident in the RSC's broadcast of *Merry Wives*, which engaged a similar disinterest in the substantiation of the commission theory. The principal interest of Laird and Klein's live interview, and of the broadcast framing overall, was in using this provenance narrative to at once excuse the apparent demerits of *Merry Wives* and to capitalise on an imagined scene of Elizabeth and Shakespeare together.

The enduring appeal of this theory, too, has its roots in the early textual examples explored in this section. It is no coincidence that – despite their different contexts and priorities – Dennis and Rowe's versions of the royal commission theory appear within a decade of each other. Michael Dobson and Nicola J. Watson, with both Dennis and Rowe in their sights, argue that the 'notion of Gloriana not just chatting familiarly with a common player but designing his most Merrie England comedy ... is far too consonant with the needs and desires of eighteenth-century cultural nationalism to be true'.[228] The same might be said of the context which prompted the RSC to focalise this fiction of the play's composition in the paratexts to the broadcast, as well as in the additional prologue scene of the production. Just as Rowe's anecdotes of Shakespeare's brushes with the law 'give a strong impression of Shakespeare', Laird's imagined iteration of the

---

[226] de Grazia, *Shakespeare without a Life*; Brian Cummings, 'Last Words: The Biographemes of Shakespeare', *Shakespeare Quarterly* 65.4 (2014): 482–490.

[227] de Grazia, *Shakespeare without a Life*, 3.

[228] Michael Dobson and Nicola J. Watson, *England's Elizabeth: An Afterlife in Fame and Fantasy* (Oxford: Oxford University Press, 2002), 122.

playwright frantically calling in favours from his fellow actors has its own narrative and imaginative virtues to supplement the apparent 'scrapp[iness]' of the play.[229]

The assumed appeal of a Shakespeare writing to royal commission is patterned in the very name of the RSC, which continually sets Shakespeare and royal authority (and, at the company's founding, another Elizabeth) in pleasant company with each other. We might wonder whether the strength of this biographical fantasy corresponds with the perceived demerits of *Merry Wives* that it is often brought forward to excuse. If this is the case, then what is perhaps most interesting is how nonspecific judgements of the play's deficiencies often are. In the case of Dennis's epistle, his principal charge against the play can be characterised as its failure to conform to the comic standards of the theatrical age Dennis was adapting for. The RSC's broadcast seemed markedly embarrassed to identify the play's defects outright, or to discuss productively the play's stereotyping of outsiders in the Windsor community. Instead, Laird and Klein's interview largely left cinema audiences to imagine what would be the product of their rushed and panicked Shakespeare, forced to call upon the improvisational talents of his fellow actors.

Like Rowe's ambiguous statement of *Merry Wives* as 'admirable Proof', the RSC broadcast of the play continued a tradition in which, on the one hand, the commission theory provides an appealing excuse for the play and, on the other, the elements of the play which *require* an excuse are left unspecified.[230] In a canon where specific forms of potential devaluation have been found – in the artistic immaturity and inconsistencies of *Two Gentlemen*, in the aesthetic excesses and jarring tonal shifts of *Titus Andronicus* – *Merry Wives* seems to buck this trend by proving that not all judgements of a play as 'substandard' within Shakespeare's elevated cultural value need to be explicitly justified from within the play itself. The historical and contemporary framing of *Merry Wives* suggests that, even when the

---

[229] de Grazia, *Shakespeare without a Life*, 3; [Live Interview] RSC Live, *The Merry Wives of Windsor*.

[230] Rowe, *Account*, vol.1, a5r.

exact demerits of the play remain obscure, they are purchased at the price of our continuing appetite for constructing compelling narratives from Shakespeare's own life.

Conclusion: 'What Is Aught, but as 'Tis Valued?'

The popular associations of Shakespeare's artistry – the elevated and even exemplary quality of his dramatic works – resist the rhetoric of apology, excuses, and explanations which accumulate within the many framing 'texts' discussed here.[231] Even as the RSC Live broadcasts locate forms of transgressive or refreshing value in these marginal plays, there is a concerted effort to align these works alongside (or, at least, in relation to) existing narratives of Shakespeare's broader cultural value, especially as these are circulated by and within British institutions. The effort it takes to align these plays – that is, to centre their fringe status – should remind us that Shakespeare's works are productively complex, and often troubling. Similarly, situating the framing of these plays for contemporary audiences alongside historical counterparts reminds us that canonical marginality can be contingent as well as long-standing.

This Element has sought to address questions which interrogate this contingency and use it to challenge the foundations of Shakespeare's value. How is a work negotiated and legitimised alongside the assumptions and associations of what counts as 'Shakespearean'? What purposes do those mediating efforts serve, and who is allowed to assume the privileged role of mediator? Which challenges remain overlooked, or unspoken, in these works? Turning these questions to the fringes of Shakespeare's body of work – in terms of canonical value, but also the fringe spaces occupied by paratexts – is essential if we are to understand more clearly how Shakespeare's place in Anglophone cultures continues to shift.

Useful challenges to Shakespeare's cultural pre-eminence reverberate throughout the plays framed in this study. The emphasis of the *Two Gentlemen* broadcast on an emphatically young Shakespeare, and on the play itself as a kind of rehearsal for his later excellence, may ostensibly

---

[231] Titular quotation is William Shakespeare, *Troilus and Cressida*, ed. Anthony B. Dawson (Cambridge: Cambridge University Press, 2017), 2.2.56.

speak to anxieties over the play's sparse performance history and a desire to spin the unfamiliarity of the play as refreshing novelty. However, there is a quieter anxiety about the threats of sexual violence, and Proteus and Valentine's treatment of Sylvia more broadly, in Sarah McRae's statement that one corollary of the play's youthful characters and energies is a concern with 'learning to understand, to forgive ... accepting what isn't perfect'.[232] This situates the framing of *Two Gentlemen* in knottier territory, suggesting that the broadcast may in fact *need* (rather than simply desire) a youthful Shakespeare to distance the more prevalent image of a mature, artistically accomplished Shakespeare from these more challenging and uncomfortable themes in the play.

The threat that these works pose may extend further than damaging ideas of Shakespeare's exemplary aesthetic qualities. The inclusion of less frequently performed plays as part of canonising projects like the RSC's may draw a greater attention to the moral, social, and political sticking points of Shakespeare's works than do the 'safer', canonically central works. The troubling elements of less frequently performed works may be subject to greater critique *because* they are staged more rarely – a phenomenon which the ever-decreasing shock value of *Titus Andronicus* seems to corroborate.[233] Greater space and attention has been afforded to engage with the complexities of Shakespeare's presentation of Blackness in *Othello* than in *Titus Andronicus*, for example, or threats of sexual violence in *Measure for Measure* than in *Two Gentlemen*. These plays thus open up productive interstices through which we might see theatre institutions attempting to mitigate Shakespeare's reputation, and to continue to justify his cultural centrality, in response to plays which have the potential to challenge it.

There is also much to be gained from a closer attention to how those elements of Shakespeare's marginal works which challenge progressive values are integrated and mediated by institutions who espouse these values in their other public-facing activities. If the RSC champions the value of

---

[232] [Pre-show Short Film] RSC Live, *The Two Gentlemen of Verona*: 00.13.11-00.13.17.

[233] See Kirwan, 'Not-Shakespeare', 98–100.

Shakespeare's works for education and access, paratexts to their broadcast activities reveal the tensions when those values brush up against the racial stereotyping of Black characters, or the silencing of female characters threatened with sexual violence. James Steichen has pointed to live theatre broadcasts as an important form of 'institutional dramaturgy' – those techniques by which 'any institution stages itself for the public'.[234] It is perhaps no surprise that Steichen's term developed in response to the 'self-documentary' quality of live theatre broadcasts.[235] (Steichen's focus, in his study, is on the Metropolitan Opera.) When the RSC streams Shakespeare's works into cinemas, it is not only the playwright whose brand and cultural identity is being performed at large. The deficient value which these paratexts have laboured to mitigate is not always exclusively Shakespeare's, as is demonstrated in Dennis and Ravenscroft's attempts to excuse the commercial failure of their own adaptations.

Stage directors, creatives, and actors who participate in live theatre broadcast paratexts may be prompted to reflect on their own challenges and failures. Genette's characterisation of the paratextual function in the printed text is often socially coded: paratexts have an 'illocutionary force', are 'present', facilitate an 'offer[ing]' of the book to readers, convey a 'commentary' and may only have an eye to 'certain readers', can 'communicate' and require a sort of 'responsibility' or even a 'commitment'.[236] The framing of Shakespeare's oft-maligned works in live theatre broadcasts creates a space in which the stakes for the pseudo-social function of the paratext could not be higher: interviews and short films which apologise, excuse, and confess to artistic failures (Shakespeare's or otherwise) are inherently personal. In this way, re-evaluating the broadcast paratext as a context in which those failures can be articulated gives these framing materials a distinctly human and vulnerable quality. Likewise, this analysis offers an opportunity to seek for the social potential in printed paratexts, too. Johnson's note on the merits and demerits of *Two Gentlemen* is, simultaneously, an exercise in his own critical dexterity and an engaged

[234] Steichen, 'HD Opera: A Love/Hate Story', 446.
[235] Steichen, 'HD Opera: A Love/Hate Story', 446.
[236] Genette, *Paratexts*, 12; 1; 2; 4; 10; 9.

critique of those commentators who preceded him. This suggests the extent to which Shakespeare's perceived deficiencies – in contexts where his cultural value is not as 'axiomatic' as in contemporary performances by the RSC – may be used to shelter (or, in Johnson's case, *expose*) the anxieties and failures of those who reproduce his works in print and performance.[237] Crucially, though, it also allows us to see the paratext as more than transactional in a commercial or semantic sense. They may be, and broadcast paratexts frequently *are*, spaces to admit of artistic and intellectual vulnerability.

This quality of broadcast paratexts is tied to the difficulty of replicating and rendering their nuances in a *purely* textual form. Attempts to negotiate Shakespeare's value against the devaluation his own works causes moments of friction and frustration which are meaningful when seen live but can be utterly flattened on the page. How does Laird's iteration of the *Merry Wives* commission theory stand against Dennis's and Rowe's if we emphasise the nervous laughter, the occasionally humorous tone, and the gestures of her interview with Suzy Klein that the broadcast's cinema audiences would have also seen? The transcribed passages used in this study have attempted to communicate as accurately as possible verbal nuances of their original – interjections, loose threads, laughter, expressions – but inevitably they capture only part of the mechanisms by which speakers in these paratexts discussed these works. What we gain in a greater sensitivity to their framing potential by approaching broadcast paratexts *as* texts is also lost in the inability to truly transcribe the intonations, pace, and non-verbal dimensions of these resources.

The same is partly true, of course, of the historical paratexts this study engages, each of which imagines a particular type of address (sometimes to the reader, sometimes with a patron in mind) being played out on in print. We might think how Johnson's first note to *Two Gentlemen* enacts an editorial sociability – if not a conversation – with those editors whose commentary he quotes, and especially with Upton. These addressees of Johnson's note may be necessarily rendered mute by the format of the edition, but does Johnson's engagement with (and critique of) their

---

[237] McLuskie and Rumbold, *Cultural Value*, 1.

positions not replicate something of the paratextual live interview, or short film? There is a peculiar irony to the fact that these paratextual engagements predate a digital age by hundreds of years, yet their retention in relation to their original 'texts' is far more stable and reliable than many of the digital materials streamed alongside these contemporary Shakespearean broadcasts.

Pascale Aebischer has suggested the extent to which '"new" performance modes are related to, and adapt the spatial configurations and modes of spectatorship that govern, early modern dramaturgies'.[238] At the core of this study is a similar conviction that live theatre broadcasts exhibit productive and unpredictable echoes of printed texts, particularly when we seek to examine the mediating impulses which have governed the (re)production of the playwright's dramatic works in different media. The framing of Shakespeare's historically devalued plays in live theatre broadcasts can, on the one hand, unsettle and destabilise narratives of the playwright's contemporary cultural value. It can also reveal to us the assumptions which underpin that value; how it is challenged; and where institutions such as the RSC meet the limit of claiming particular plays as 'Shakespearean'. In this sense, live theatre broadcast paratexts, like their printed counterparts, are deeply transitional. They are spaces for negotiating error, discomfort, for apology, and excusal. They are, in short, where we see the minute boundaries of the Shakespearean canon being reconstituted in real time.

---

[238] Pascale Aebischer, *Shakespeare, Spectatorship, and the Technologies of Performance* (Cambridge: Cambridge University Press, 2020), 3.

Appendix: *The Two Gentlemen of Verona* (2014) Broadcast Transcript

The following is a partial transcript of the pre-show presenter monologue and pre-show short film broadcast as part of RSC Live's *Two Gentlemen of Verona* (originally broadcast 3 September 2014). It does not reproduce these paratexts in their entirety but is a partial reconstruction based on transcript notes from the RSC's internal archival copy.

Time stamps are included to refer to the points at which these paratexts commenced in the broadcast's live transmission.

Punctuation has been added in places to aid written comprehension, including en dashes to signify a pause or shift in tone in the middle of a locution. Insertions in square brackets may be used to signify absent words, or to offer a conjectural word where the original is not discernible.

SK: Suzy Klein, broadcast presenter.
SG: Simon Godwin, director of the stage production of *The Two Gentlemen of Verona*.
MM: Michael Marcus (Valentine).
SM: Sarah McRae (Sylvia).
MA: Mark Arends (Proteus).
PC: Pearl Chanda (Julia).

<u>00:03:56–00:06.02 Live feed from theatre interior begins; SK delivers her presenter monologue from onstage, the scene is set as a café in Verona. Pre-set action includes actors onstage behind Klein.</u>

SK: Obsession, jealousy, friendship and love – we have a lot to look forward to this evening. A very warm welcome to Stratford-upon-Avon for tonight's sell-out show. It has been forty-four years since the Royal Shakespeare Company last presented The Two Gentlemen of Verona here on the mainstage and it remains one of Shakespeare's least known plays. So we asked director Simon Godwin along with some of the members of the cast of this glittering new production to tell us a bit about the story and the characters.

00:06:03–00:14.01 Pre-recorded short film.

SG: Very briefly, the plot of The Two Gentlemen of Verona is: 'Man falls in love with his best friend's girlfriend.' It's a Shakespearean romcom with dark edges. It's about young people; so the four protagonists are all young. And it's a play about feeling things for the first time, about falling in love for the first time and how unbelievably intense that feels. And a lot of the play is about what you do with a feeling that is so towering, so completely overpowering that you're willing to risk everything and you're willing to risk friendship and family and even your life for the strength of your feeling.

MM: Valentine is one of the gentlemen of Verona – [he] doesn't quite know where he is and is – sort of – [he] seems to be running away from something rather than going towards something but I think tries to convince himself that actually it's what he wants is out there in Milan and not at home. I think just the different encounters that he has with the different characters whether it be his lifelong friend in Proteus or his new-found love in Sylvia or dealing with the Duke and [to] experience what it's like to suddenly be in love and suddenly not to be able to be with the person that you love.

SG: Who is Sylvia? That's the title of the song that one of her many suitors sings to her during the play. So, she's had a privileged background: lots of suitors have appealed to her heart and yet when she falls for this man, Valentine, she gives him one hundred per cent and she shows the other characters what love can be. I mean, generally, the women in the play are much more reliable, consistent, and, if you like, heroic than the men.

SM: She meets this guy from Verona called Valentine, who is probably unlike anyone else she had met before, in her very closeted world of – in our production – Gucci bags and Prada [laughs] and [she] completely falls for him, very quickly, and decides to turn her back on everything including her father. And I think the Duke had a line about how she has rejected all of my possessions as being worthless and she turns her back on all of that to go and – into a very dangerous forest – to find the guy that she loves and go and marry him and be poor, and be happy. Uhm, and – that's what she wants to do – it doesn't go quite that well [laughs].

SG: Proteus is – well, there's a bit of Proteus in all of us, his name implies changeability – 'untrustworthy' would be a view but equally you might just say he's drawn from one place to another. He's ambitious, and he has a strong sense that whatever anyone else has, he too should have.

MA: In the early scenes of this play, Proteus by all accounts seems like a nice guy – what people say about him, Valentine says, what Julia says about him. He seems – there's no reason to suspect that he might do the things that he does. And then when he makes these very rash and slightly outrageous choices so quickly, there's real [fun?] in making those choices and I think sometimes the audience really enjoys watching a character behave so badly, especially one that they've come to expect would behave so well.

SG: If Proteus transforms, then Julia transforms in a very different way. She is the girl who's left at home when Proteus leaves to go to Milan, she follows him to Milan but not as herself but in disguise.

PC: Julia is a girl who lives in Verona and she is in love with Proteus. She becomes engaged with Proteus just before he goes to Milan and she misses him so much when he's gone that she decides that she's gonna go to Milan and she's gonna go to Milan dressed as a boy. When she gets to Milan, she finds that Proteus has fallen in love with another woman and she's stuck dressed as a boy and has to kind of try and figure out a way of getting him back.

SG: One of the things the play's most famous for is the presence of a dog. His name is Crab and he's more than a dog, he's a character, with an attitude, with action, with an impact on the plot. He's kind of the star of the show. I don't think I'd realised that it's true that really, dogs are not actors – I mean, I sort of had this fantasy I would talk to the dog about – you know, the character and negotiate a little bit. And then you realise the dog is interested in treats, what the trainer of the dog calls 'payment', which is essentially chocolate dog drops and so that's the discourse: give the dog a treat and pray the dog will do what you want the dog to do. Shakespeare locates the play in Italy. He does that, I think, to access a passionate, hot-blooded quality. So Verona, for him, represents this fiery, exciting, charged place: so we start there and then we travel to Milan. And if Verona is charged and passionate, well Milan is that plus plus plus plus plus plus. So what I've tried to do in the show is make Verona a place where you feel kind of familiar and relaxed and at ease, and Milan is somewhere you feel a little bit thrilled by. The wilderness – and often, in Shakespeare, he creates a landscape where people will undergo change psychological change as well as physical change. And here in the play, which is so much, actually, about growing up; you start at the home, you travel to the city, and you arrive at a liminal wilderness forest in which your real emotions and your real self can be found, and ultimately worked through.

MM: It's been really nice to work on a play that was written by a young writer, writing about young people. It was very early on in Shakespeare's career and so, you kind of see this writer who's clearly got quite profound thoughts and a really unique insight into the world and into playwriting but in some areas has not quite developed those thoughts and ideas yet but will do throughout his career.

SM: Probably because he was very young when he wrote it as well, I think it is a kind of coming of age, growing up and accepting what isn't perfect [narrative]. And I think it's a lot about being in love and what that means – and yeah, learning to understand, to forgive and uhm, yeah, things won't be perfect but that's part of growing up.

SG: One of the prerequisites of directing a play, hopefully, well is that you fall in love with it – so now of course I'm the biggest supporter of the play there is and I can't believe it hasn't been done for so long and I can't wait for it to be done again. The flipside of that is,

I was delighted that it hadn't been done for so long because there isn't that historical baggage that can feel so intimidating: everyone comparing that production to the one that they've seen the year before or the actors knowing people that have played their own parts or carrying those kind of cultural memories. There's no baggage with this. The themes of desire, and justice, and growing up will never leave us and so I don't think the play will ever leave us either.

References

Aebischer, Pascale and Susanne Greenhalgh, 'Introduction: Shakespeare and the "Live" Theatre Broadcast Experience', in *Shakespeare and the 'Live' Theatre Broadcast Experience*, eds. Aebischer, Greenhalgh and Laurie E. Osbourne (London: Bloomsbury, 2017), 1–16.

Aebischer, Pascale, *Shakespeare, Spectatorship, and the Technologies of Performance* (Cambridge: Cambridge University Press, 2020).

Akhimie, Patricia, 'Racist Humour and Shakespearean Comedy', *The Cambridge Companion to Shakespeare and Race*, ed. Ayanna Thompson (Cambridge: Cambridge University Press, 2021), 47–61.

August, Hannah, 'Text/Paratext', in *Shakespeare / Text*, ed. Claire M. L. Bourne (London: Bloomsbury, 2021), 50–65.

Barker, Martin, *Live to your Local Cinema: The Remarkable Rise of Livecasting* (London: Palgrave, 2014).

Bate, Jonathan, 'The RSC Complete Works Festival: An Introduction and Retrospective', *Shakespeare* 3.2 (2007), 183–188.

Bate, Jonathan, ed. *Titus Andronicus*, Revised 3rd ed. (London: Bloomsbury, 2018).

Bate, Jonathan, and Eric Rasmussen, eds. *The RSC Shakespeare: The Complete Works*, 2nd ed. (London: Bloomsbury, 2022).

Bennett, Susan, *Performing Nostalgia: Shifting Shakespeare and the Contemporary Past* (London: Routledge Press, 1996).

Bowdler, Thomas, ed. *The Family Shakespeare*, 10 vols. (London: Longman, 1818).

Brown, David Sterling, *Shakespeare's White Others* (Cambridge: Cambridge University Press, 2023).

Burgess-Van Aken, Barbara, 'Contexts of Fear: Edward Ravenscroft's Adaptation of Shakespeare's *Titus Andronicus*', *Actes des Congres de la Societe Francaise Shakespeare* 36 (2018), 1–14.

Caines, Michael, *Shakespeare and the Eighteenth Century* (Oxford: Oxford University Press, 2013).

Chambers, Colin, *Inside the Royal Shakespeare Company: Creativity and the Institution* (London: Taylor and Francis, 2004).

Crane, David, ed. *The Merry Wives of Windsor*, 2nd ed. (Cambridge: Cambridge University Press, 2010).

Cummings, Brian, 'Last Words: The Biographemes of Shakespeare', *Shakespeare Quarterly* 65.4 (2014), 482–490.

Dawson, Anthony B. ed. *Troilus and Cressida*, 2nd ed. (Cambridge: Cambridge University Press, 2017).

de Grazia, Margareta, *Shakespeare Verbatim: The Reproduction of Authenticity in the 1790 Apparatus* (Oxford: Oxford University Press, 1991).

de Grazia, Margareta, *Shakespeare without a Life* (Oxford: Oxford University Press, 2023).

Dennis, John, *The Comical Gallant: or, the Amours of Sir John Falstaffe. A Comedy, as it is Acted at the Theatre Royal in Drury-Lane. By his Majestie's Servants. By Mr Dennis. To which is added, a large Account of the Taste in Poetry, and the Causes of the Degeneracy of It* (London: A. Baldwin, 1702).

Dennis, John, *An Essay on the Genius and Writings of Shakespear: With Some Letters of Criticism to the Spectator* (London: Bernard Lintott, 1712).

Depledge, Emma, *Shakespeare's Rise to Cultural Prominence: Politics, Print and Alteration, 1642–1700* (Cambridge: Cambridge University Press, 2018).

Dobson, Michael, *The Making of the National Poet: Shakespeare, Adaptation, and Authorship, 1660–1769* (Oxford: Oxford University Press, 1994).

Dobson, Michael, 'Bowdler and Britannia: Shakespeare and the National Libido', *Shakespeare Survey* 46 (2007), 137–144.

Dobson, Michael, 'Watching the Complete Works Festival: The RSC and Its Fans in 2006', *Shakespeare Bulletin* 25.4 (Winter 2007), 23–33.

Dobson, Michael and Nicola J. Watson, *England's Elizabeth: An Afterlife in Fame and Fantasy* (Oxford: Oxford University Press, 2002).

Edwards, Philip, ed. *Hamlet, Prince of Denmark* (Cambridge: Cambridge University Press, 2019).

Erne, Lukas, *Shakespeare and the Book Trade* (Cambridge: Cambridge University Press, 2013).

Genette, Gérard, *Paratexts: Thresholds of Interpretation*, trans. by Jane E. Lewin (Cambridge: Cambridge University Press, 1997).

Greenblatt, Stephen, *Shakespearean Negotiations: The Circulation of Social Energy in Renaissance England* (Berkley: University of California Press, 1988).

Hamm, Robert B., 'Rowe's "Shakespear" (1709) and the Tonson House Style', *College Literature* 31.3 (2004), 179–205.

Hawkes, Rebecca, 'Live Broadcast of Benedict Cumberbatch's *Hamlet* Watched by 225,000 People', *The Telegraph*, 21 October 2015, www.telegraph.co.uk/theatre/what-to-see/benedict-cumberbatch-hamlet-live/ [accessed 3 March 2023].

Hawkins, Ella, *Shakespeare in Elizabethan Costume: 'Period Dress' in Twenty-First Century Performance* (London: Bloomsbury, 2022).

Holland, Peter, 'Openings', in *Shakespeare and the Making of Theatre*, eds. Stuart Hampton-Reeves and Bridget Escolme (Basingstoke: Palgrave Macmillan, 2012), 14–31.

Hooks, Adam G., *Selling Shakespeare: Biography, Bibliography and the Book Trade* (Cambridge: Cambridge University Press, 2016).

Hughes, Alan, ed. *Titus Andronicus* (Cambridge: Cambridge University Press, 2006).

Hutchison, David, 'Benedict Cumberbatch *Hamlet* Takes £3m at NT Live Box Office', *The Stage*, 9 December 2015, www.thestage.co.uk/news/benedict-cumberbatch-hamlet-takes-3m-at-nt-live-box-office [accessed 3 March 2023].

Internet Movie Database, 'William Shakespeare (1564–1616)', www.imdb.com/name/nm0000636/ [accessed 15 July 2024].

Jarvis, Simon, *Scholars and Gentlemen: Shakespearean Textual Criticism and Representations of Scholarly Labour, 1725–1765* (Oxford: Oxford University Press, 1995).

Johnson, Samuel, ed. *The Plays of William Shakespeare*, 8 vols. (London: J. and R. Tonson et al., 1765).

Karim-Cooper, Farah, ed. *Titus Andronicus: The State of Play* (London: Bloomsbury, 2019).

Kirwan, Peter, '"You Have No Voice!": Constructing Reputation through Contemporaries in the Shakespeare Biopic', *Shakespeare Bulletin* 32.1 (Spring 2014), 11–26.

Kirwan, Peter, 'Not-Shakespeare and the Shakespearean Ghost', in *The Oxford Handbook of Shakespeare and Performance*, ed. James C. Bulman (Oxford: Oxford University Press, 2017), 87–103.

Kirwan, Peter, '"Complete" Works: The Folio and All of Shakespeare', *The Cambridge Companion to Shakespeare's First Folio*, ed. Emma Smith (Cambridge: Cambridge University Press, 2016), 86–102.

Kitzes, Adam H., 'The Hazards of Expurgation: Adapting *Measure for Measure* to the Bowdler *Family Shakespeare*', *Journal for Early Modern Cultural Studies* 13.2 (2013), 43–68.

Kitzes, Adam H., 'John Dennis and the Shakespeare-Elizabeth Anecdote: *The Comical Gallant* and the Reception of *The Merry Wives of Windsor*', *Restoration and 18th Century Theatre Research* 28.2 (Winter 2013), 45–70.

Laingbane, Gerard, *An Account of the English Dramatick Poets, or, Some Observations and Remarks on the Lives and Writings of All Those That Have Publish'd either Comedies, Tragedies, Tragi-Comedies, Pastorals, Masques, Interludes, Farces or Opera's in the English Tongue* (Oxford: Printed by L. L. for George West and Henry Clements, 1691).

Loomba, Ania, *Shakespeare, Race, and Colonialism* (Oxford: Oxford University Press, 2002).

Loughnane, Rory, 'Shakespeare and the Idea of Early Authorship', *Early Shakespeare: 1588–1594*, eds. Rory Loughnane and Andrew J. Power (Cambridge: Cambridge University Press, 2020), 21–53.

Loughnane, Rory and Andrew J. Power, eds. *Early Shakespeare: 1588–1594* (Cambridge: Cambridge University Press, 2020), 1–20.

Maguire, Laurie, and Emma Smith, 'Theater, Revision, and *The Merry Wives of Windsor*', *Shakespeare Quarterly* 72.3–4 (2022), 177–202.

McLuskie, Kate, and Kate Rumbold, *Cultural Value in Twenty-First Century England: The Case of Shakespeare* (Manchester: Manchester University Press, 2017).

Murphy, Andrew, *Shakespeare in Print: A History and Chronology of Shakespeare Publishing*, 2nd ed. (Cambridge: Cambridge University Press, 2021).

National Theatre Live, *King Lear*, directed for the screen by Robin Lough, Donmar Warehouse Theatre, London, 3 February 2011.

Neville, Sarah, ed. *The Merry Wives of Windsor* (Oxford: Oxford University Press, 2024).

Newman, Harry, 'Paratexts and Canonical Thresholds', *Shakespeare* 13.4 (2017), 313–317.

Nicholas, Rachael, 'Encountering Shakespeare Elsewhere: Digital Distribution, Audience Reception, and the Changing Value of Shakespeare in Performance' (Doctoral Thesis, University of Roehampton, 2019).

Nicholls, John, ed. *Illustrations of the Literary History of the Eighteenth Century*, 8 vols. (London: Nichols, Son and Bentley, 1817–1858).

Olive, Sarah, *Shakespeare Valued: Educational Policy and Pedagogy 1998–2009* (Bristol: Intellect, 2015).

Oxford Cambridge and RSA (OCR), *GCSE English Literature J352/22 Shakespeare (8 June 2022)* www.ocr.org.uk/Images/685747-question-paper-shakespeare.pdf [accessed 5 July 2023].

Pope, Alexander, ed. *The Works of Shakespear in Six Volumes, Collated and Corrected by Former Editions, by Mr Pope*, 6 vols. (London: Jacob Tonson, 1725).

Preiss, Richard, *Clowning and Authorship in Early Modern England* (Cambridge: Cambridge University Press, 2014).

Price, Eoin, 'Canon: Framing Not-Shakespearean Performance', in *The Arden Research Handbook of Shakespeare and Contemporary Performance*, eds. Peter Kirwan and Kathyrn Prince (London: Bloomsbury, 2021), 151–170.

Purcell, Stephen, *Shakespeare and Audience in Practice* (London: Ardem Bloomsbury, 2013).

Ravenscroft, Edward, *Titus Andronicus, or, The Rape of Lavinia* (London: J Hindmarsh, 1687).

Rowe, Nicholas, ed. *The Works of Mr. William Shakespear*, 6 vols. (London: Jacob Tonson, 1709).

Royal Shakespeare Company, *The Two Gentlemen of Verona*, directed by Simon Godwin, The Royal Shakespeare Theatre, Stratford-upon-Avon, 2014.

Royal Shakespeare Company, *Titus Andronicus*, directed by Blanche McIntyre, The Royal Shakespeare Theatre, Stratford-upon-Avon, 2017.

Royal Shakespeare Company, *The Merry Wives of Windsor*, directed by Fiona Laird, The Royal Shakespeare Theatre, Stratford-upon-Avon, 2018.

Royster, Francesca T., 'White-Limed Walls: Whiteness and Gothic Extremism in Shakespeare's *Titus Andronicus*', *Shakespeare Quarterly* 51.4 (2000), 432–455.

RSC Live from Stratford-upon-Avon, *The Two Gentlemen of Verona*, directed for the screen by Robin Lough, Royal Shakespeare Theatre, Stratford-upon-Avon, 3 September 2014.

RSC Live from Stratford-upon-Avon, *Othello*, directed for the screen by Robin Lough, Royal Shakespeare Theatre, Stratford-upon-Avon, 25 August 2015.

RSC Live from Stratford-upon-Avon, *Hamlet*, directed for the screen by Robin Lough, Royal Shakespeare Theatre, Stratford-upon-Avon, 8 June 2016.

RSC Live from Stratford-upon-Avon, *Titus Andronicus*, directed for the screen by Matthew Woodward, Royal Shakespeare Theatre, Stratford-upon-Avon, 9 August 2017.

RSC Live from Stratford-upon-Avon, *The Merry Wives of Windsor*, directed for the screen by Dewi Humphreys, Royal Shakespeare Theatre, Stratford-upon-Avon, 12 September 2018.

Rumbold, Kate, 'Brand Shakespeare?', *Shakespeare Survey* 64 (2011), 25–37.

Scheil, Katherine West, *The Taste of the Town: Shakespearian Comedy and the Early Eighteenth Century Theater* (London: Associated University Presses, 2003).

Schlueter, Kurt, ed. *The Two Gentlemen of Verona* (Cambridge: Cambridge University Press, 2012).

Schoenbaum, Samuel, *Shakespeare's Lives* 2nd ed. (Oxford: Clarendon Press, 1991).

Seary, Peter, *Lewis Theobald and the Editing of Shakespeare* (Oxford: Clarendon Press, 1990).

Sharpe, Will, *Shakespeare and Collaborative Writing* (Oxford: Oxford University Press, 2023).

Sharrock, Beth, 'Framing Shakespeare in New Digital Canons: Paratextual Conventions of RSC Live and NT Live', *Shakespeare Bulletin* 40.2 (2022), 239–265.

Shakespeare, William, *A Most Pleasant and Excellent Conceited Comedie, of Syr John Falstaffe, and the Merrie Wives of Windsor* (London: Arthur Johnson, 1602)

Sherbo, Arthur, 'George Steevens's 1785 Variorum "Shakespeare"', *Studies in Bibliography*, 32 (1979), 241–246.

Sherlock, Peter. 'Arundell, Henry, Third Baron Arundell of Wardour (bap. 1608, d. 1694), Royalist Army Officer and Politician'. *Oxford Dictionary of National Biography*. 21. Oxford University Press. [Accessed 13 May 2023] www.oxforddnb.com/view/10.1093/ref:odnb/9780198614128.001.0001/odnb-9780198614128-e-716.

Spencer, Hazelton, *Shakespeare Improved: The Restoration Versions in Quarto and on the Stage* (New York: Frederick Ungar, 1927), 287–292.

Steichen, James, 'HD Opera: A Love/Hate Story', *Opera Quarterly* 27.4 (2011), 443–459.

Stern, Tiffany, *Documents of Performance in Early Modern England* (Cambridge: Cambridge University Press, 2009).

Sullivan, Erin, 'The Audience is Present: Aliveness, Social Media, and the Theatre Broadcast Experience', in *Shakespeare and the 'Live' Theatre Broadcast Experience*, eds. Pascale Aebischer, Susanne Greenhalgh and Laurie E. Osborne (London: Bloomsbury, 2018), 59–76.

Sullivan, Erin, *Shakespeare and Digital Performance in Practice* (London: Palgrave, 2022).

Taylor, Gary, *Reinventing Shakespeare: A Cultural History from the Restoration to the Present* (London: Hogarth Press, 1989).

Taylor, Gary, and Rory Loughnane, 'The Canon and Chronology', in *The New Oxford Shakespeare: Authorship Companion*, eds. Gary Taylor and Gabriel Egan (Oxford: Oxford University Press, 2017), 417–602.

Thompson, Ayanna Tene, *Depicting Race and Torture on the Early Modern Stage* (Doctoral Thesis, Harvard University, 2001).

Upton, John, *Critical Observations on Shakespeare*, 2nd ed. (London: G Hawkins, 1748).

Waith, Eugene M, ed. *Titus Andronicus* (Oxford: Oxford University Press, 1984).

Walsh, Marcus, *Shakespeare, Milton, and Eighteenth-Century Literary Editing: The Beginnings of Interpretive Scholarship* (Cambridge: Cambridge University Press, 1997).

Walsh, Marcus, 'George Steevens and the 1778 Variorum: A Hermeneutics and a Social Economy of Annotation', in *Shakespeare and the Eighteenth Century*, eds. Peter Sabor and Paul Yachnin (Hampshire: Ashgate, 2008), 71–83.

Walsh, Marcus, 'Editing and Publishing Shakespeare', in *Shakespeare in the Eighteenth Century*, eds. Fiona Ritchie and Peter Sabor (Cambridge: Cambridge University Press, 2012), 21–40.

Warburton, William, ed. *The Works of Shakespear*, 8. vols. (London: J. and P. Knapton, 1747).

Warren, Roger, ed. *The Two Gentlemen of Verona* (Oxford: Oxford University Press, 2008).

Watson, Carly, 'From Restorer to Editor: The Evolution of Lewis Theobald's Textual Critical Practice', *The Library* 20.2 (2019), 147–171.

Way, Geoffrey, 'Together, Apart: Liveness, Eventness, and Streaming Shakesperean Performance', *Shakespeare Bulletin* 35.3 (2017), 389–406.

Wells, Stanley, '*The Failure of the Two Gentlemen of Verona*', *Shakespeare Jarbuch* 99 (1963), 161–173.

Whipday, Emma, '"The Picture of a Woman": Roaring Girls and Alternative Histories in the RSC 2014 Season', *Shakespeare* 11.3 (2015), 272–285.

Wyver, John, 'Screening the RSC Stage: The 2014 Live from Stratford-upon-Avon Cinema Broadcasts', *Shakespeare* 11.3 (2015), 286–302.

Wyver, John, *Screening the Royal Shakespeare Company: A Critical History* (London: Bloomsbury, 2019).

Yarn, Molly, *Shakespeare's 'Lady Editors': A New History of the Shakespearean Text* (Cambridge: Cambridge University Press, 2022).

Acknowledgements

This Element began its life as a chapter of my doctoral thesis, which was nurtured at every stage by Peter Kirwan and Erin Sullivan. I am grateful to John Wyver for generously sharing access to broadcast transmissions from the Royal Shakespeare Company. I have also benefitted from the support of Midlands4Cities, who funded this research in its doctoral and postdoctoral iterations. As general editors to this series, Claire M. L. Bourne and Rory Loughnane have helped to shape this work with careful attention and patience. My sincere thanks are due to them, and to the two reviewers of the manuscript, for their thoughtful suggestions. Speaking from the margins of this Element with love and erudition are Felicity Brown, Anouska Lester, and Dylan Wright. My greatest debt is always to my family – there is no question of their value.

Cambridge Elements⁼

Shakespeare and Text

Claire M. L. Bourne
The Pennsylvania State University

Claire M. L. Bourne is Associate Professor of English at The Pennsylvania State University. She is author of *Typographies of Performance in Early Modern England* (Oxford University Press 2020) and editor of the collection *Shakespeare / Text* (Bloomsbury 2021). She has published extensively on early modern book design and reading practices in venues such as *PBSA*, *ELR*, *Shakespeare*, and numerous edited collections. She is also co-author (with Jason Scott-Warren) of an article attributing the annotations in the Free Library of Philadelphia's copy of the Shakespeare First Folio to John Milton. She has edited Fletcher and Massinger's *The Sea Voyage* for the *Routledge Anthology of Early Modern Drama* (2020) and is working on an edition of *Henry the Sixth, Part 1* for the Arden Shakespeare, Fourth Series.

Rory Loughnane
University of Kent

Rory Loughnane is Reader in Early Modern Studies and Co-director of the Centre for Medieval and Early Modern Studies at the University of Kent. He is the author or editor of nine books and has published widely on Shakespeare and textual studies. In his role as Associate Editor of the New Oxford Shakespeare, he has edited more than ten of Shakespeare's plays, and co-authored with Gary Taylor a book-length study about the 'Canon and Chronology' of Shakespeare's works. He is a General Editor of the forthcoming

Oxford Marlowe edition, a Series Editor of Studies in Early Modern Authorship (Routledge), a General Editor of the *CADRE* database (cadredb.net), and a General Editor of The Revels Plays series (Manchester University Press).

ADVISORY BOARD

Patricia Akhimie
The Folger Institute
Terri Bourus
Florida State University
Dennis Britton
University of British Columbia
Miles P. Grier
Queen's College, City University of New York
Chiaki Hanabusa
Keio University
Sujata Iyengar
University of Georgia
Jason Scott-Warren
University of Cambridge

M. J. Kidnie
University of Western Ontario
Zachary Lesser
University of Pennsylvania
Tara L. Lyons
Illinois State University
Joyce MacDonald
University of Kentucky
Laurie Maguire
Magdalen College, University of Oxford
David McInnis
University of Melbourne
Iolanda Plescia
Sapienza – University of Rome
Alan Stewart
Columbia University

ABOUT THE SERIES

Cambridge Elements in Shakespeare and Text offers a platform for original scholarship about the creation, circulation, reception, remaking, use, performance, teaching, and translation of the Shakespearean text across time and place. The series seeks to publish research that challenges – and pushes beyond – the conventional parameters of Shakespeare and textual studies.

Cambridge Elements⁼

Shakespeare and Text

ELEMENTS IN THE SERIES

Shakespeare, Malone and the Problems of Chronology
Tiffany Stern

Theatre History, Attribution Studies, and the Question of Evidence
Holger Schott Syme

Facsimiles and the History of Shakespeare Editing
Paul Salzman

Editing Archipelagic Shakespeare
Rory Loughnane and Willy Maley

Shakespeare Broadcasts and the Question of Value
Beth Sharrock

A full series listing is available at: www.cambridge.org/ESTX

For EU product safety concerns, contact us at Calle de José Abascal, 56–1°, 28003 Madrid, Spain or eugpsr@cambridge.org.

www.ingramcontent.com/pod-product-compliance
Lightning Source LLC
LaVergne TN
LVHW020349260326
834688LV00045B/1617